Key to Symbols

 This is a guide to each recipe's preparation and cooking.

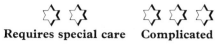

| **Easy** | **Requires special care** | **Complicated** |

 This is a guide to the cost of each dish and will, of course, vary according to region and season.

Inexpensive   **Reasonable**   **Expensive**

This is a guide to the preparation and cooking time required for each dish and will vary according to the skill of the individual cook.

Less than 1 hour   **1 hour to 2½ hours**   **Over 2½ hours**

British Ingredients — American Equivalents

British Ingredients	American Equivalents
Castor sugar	Fine sugar
Icing sugar	Confectioners', or powdered, sugar
100% wholemeal flour	Wholewheat flour
Cornflour	Cornstarch
Sultana	Raisin
Desiccated coconut	Shredded coconut
Black treacle	Molasses
Bicarbonate of soda	Baking soda
Single cream	Light cream
Double cream	Heavy cream
Biscuit	Cookie
Digestive biscuit	Graham cracker
Scone	Biscuit
Sweet	Candy
Tart	Pie
Tomato chutney	Chili sauce
Gammon slice	Ham steak
Minced beef	Ground beef
Spring onion	Scallion
Potato crisp	Potato chip
Potato chip	French fried potato

Oven Temperatures

	Fahrenheit	Centigrade	Gas
Very cool	250°F	130°C	Gas Mark ½
	275°F	140°C	Gas Mark 1
Cool	300°F	150°C	Gas Mark 2
Warm	325°F	170°C	Gas Mark 3
Moderate	350°F	180°C	Gas Mark 4
Fairly hot	375°F	190°C	Gas Mark 5
	400°F	200°C	Gas Mark 6
Hot	425°F	220°C	Gas Mark 7
Very hot	450°F	230°C	Gas Mark 8
	475°F	240°C	Gas Mark 9
	500°F	250°C	Gas Mark 10

To convert Fahrenheit into Centigrade:
    subtract 32, multiply by 5, divide by 9
To convert Centigrade into Fahrenheit:
    multiply by 9, divide by 5, add 32

Solid Measures

28.352 grams = 1 ounce, but for convenience we have rounded it up to 30 grams

15 grams	= ½ ounce
30 grams	= 1 ounce
60 grams	= 2 ounces
75 grams	= 2½ ounces
100 grams	= 3½ ounces
500 grams	= 1 pound, 1½ ounces
1 kilogram = 1,000 grams	= 2 pounds, 3 ounces

Liquid Measures

Metric		British	American
1 litre	= 1,000 millilitres	= 1¾ pints	= 4½ cups
1 demilitre	= 500 millilitres	= 17 fluid ounces (generous)	= 2 cups
1 decilitre	= 100 millilitres	= 4 fluid ounces	= ½ cup
	15 millilitres	= ½ fluid ounce	= 1 tablespoon
	5 millilitres	= 1 teaspoon	= 1 teaspoon
British Imperial pint		= 20 fluid ounces	
American pint		= 16 fluid ounces	
1 British cup		= ½ pint = 10 fluid ounces	
1 American cup		= ½ pint = 8 fluid ounces	

Linear Measures

25 millimetres (2½ centimetres)	=	1 inch
305 millimetres (30½ centimetres)	=	1 foot
1 metre (100 centimetres)	=	40 inches

Equivalents for Basic Foods

		British	American	Metric
Breadcrumbs—dry		3 ounces	1 cup	90 grams
	fresh	2 ounces	1 cup	60 grams
Butter		½ ounce	1 tablespoon	15 grams
		4 ounces	½ cup	120 grams
		1 pound	2 cups	480 grams
Cheese, grated		4 ounces	1 cup	120 grams
Cornflour [Cornstarch]		¼ ounce	1 tablespoon	7 grams
Plain [All purpose] **flour**		1 ounce	¼ cup	30 grams
		2 ounces	½ cup	60 grams
		4 ounces	1 cup	120 grams
		1 pound	3 cups	480 grams
Self-raising flour		1 ounce	¼ cup	30 grams
		2 ounces	½ cup	60 grams
		4 ounces	1 cup	120 grams
Raisins, seedless		⅓ ounce	1 tablespoon	10 grams
		6 ounces	1 cup	180 grams
		1 pound	1⅔ cups	480 grams
Rice (uncooked)		6 ounces	1 cup	180 grams
Castor [fine] **sugar**		½ ounce	1 tablespoon	15 grams
		4 ounces	½ cup	120 grams
		8 ounces	1 cup	240 grams
Brown sugar		⅓ ounce	1 tablespoon	10 grams
		3 ounces	½ cup	90 grams
		6 ounces	1 cup	180 grams

All weight and measure equivalents are approximate
Tablespoons and teaspoons are standard British measures

THE HOME BREAD BAKER

ARCO PUBLISHING COMPANY, INC.
New York

Editor: Yvonne Deutch

Photographs: Roger Phillips 6-16, 22-32, 36/7, 40-43,
48-53, 55, 58, 61(top), 62, 64-67, 70, 71, covers.
Alan Duns: 17, 47, 59, 60, 61
David Meldrum: 19, 46, 63
Paul Kemp: 20/1, 45
Iain Reid: 34, 57
Gina Harris: 54, 68
Rex Bamber: 38/9

Published 1975 by Arco Publishing Company, Inc.
219 Park Avenue South, New York, N.Y. 10003

© Marshall Cavendish Publications Ltd. 1975

This material was first published by
Marshall Cavendish Ltd. in the partwork Supercook

Library of Congress Catalog Card Number 74-14119

ISBN 0-668-03640-0

Printed in Great Britain by Severn Valley Press

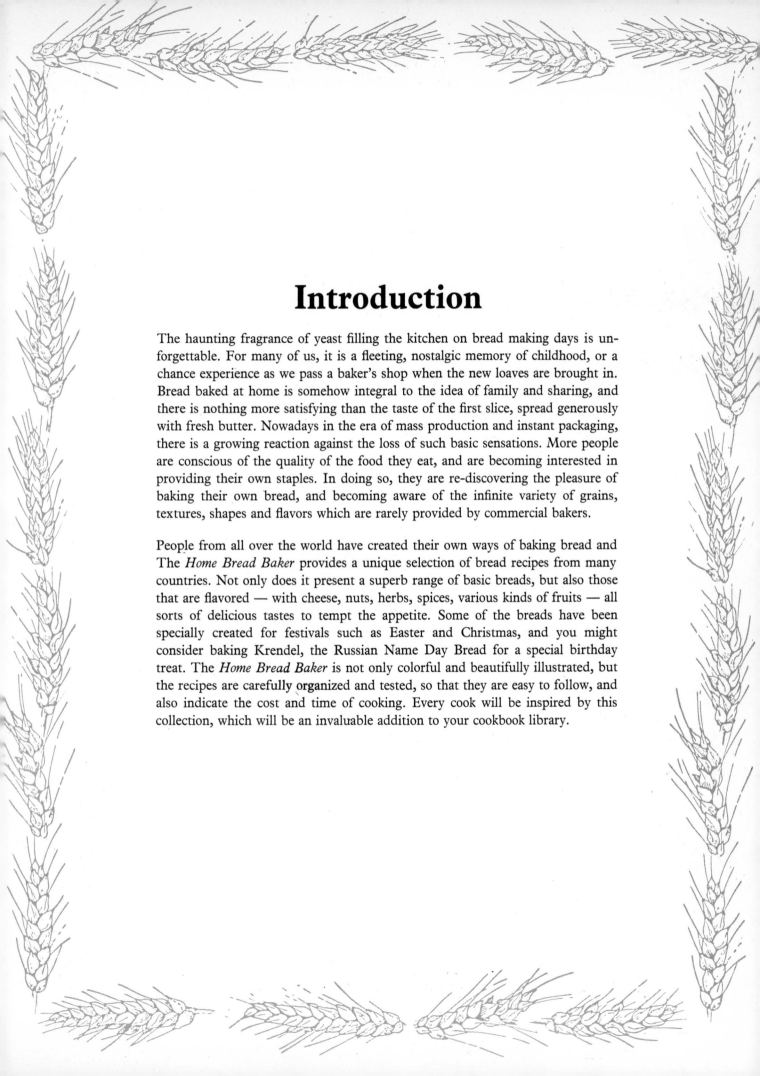

Introduction

The haunting fragrance of yeast filling the kitchen on bread making days is unforgettable. For many of us, it is a fleeting, nostalgic memory of childhood, or a chance experience as we pass a baker's shop when the new loaves are brought in. Bread baked at home is somehow integral to the idea of family and sharing, and there is nothing more satisfying than the taste of the first slice, spread generously with fresh butter. Nowadays in the era of mass production and instant packaging, there is a growing reaction against the loss of such basic sensations. More people are conscious of the quality of the food they eat, and are becoming interested in providing their own staples. In doing so, they are re-discovering the pleasure of baking their own bread, and becoming aware of the infinite variety of grains, textures, shapes and flavors which are rarely provided by commercial bakers.

People from all over the world have created their own ways of baking bread and The *Home Bread Baker* provides a unique selection of bread recipes from many countries. Not only does it present a superb range of basic breads, but also those that are flavored — with cheese, nuts, herbs, spices, various kinds of fruits — all sorts of delicious tastes to tempt the appetite. Some of the breads have been specially created for festivals such as Easter and Christmas, and you might consider baking Krendel, the Russian Name Day Bread for a special birthday treat. The *Home Bread Baker* is not only colorful and beautifully illustrated, but the recipes are carefully organized and tested, so that they are easy to follow, and also indicate the cost and time of cooking. Every cook will be inspired by this collection, which will be an invaluable addition to your cookbook library.

Contents

Bread-making

It is easy to buy a commercially made loaf of bread or even freshly baked bread from a bakery, but neither of these will give you the sense of satisfaction you will have when your family and friends tuck into a loaf of bread you have made yourself.

Making bread is an art, but, contrary to some opinion, it can be easily mastered. Bread recipes vary considerably and the general guidelines set out here will not fit all of them exactly, but if you understand what each ingredient is meant to do and what the techniques are, you will be on your way to successful bread-making.

INGREDIENTS

Flour

The type, or types, of flour you use for your bread is really a matter of personal taste, but the best flours for both bread and yeast doughs are milled from hard wheat. These flours have a high gluten content which produces a more elastic springy dough, while soft-wheat flours make a rather sticky dough.

Almost all the white flour sold commercially is soft household flour. Health food stores, however, usually stock wholewheat flour, stone-ground flour, 100 percent wholemeal flour (the whole grain of the wheat with nothing removed and nothing added) and 85 percent or 90 percent wholemeal flour (the husk and the bran removed). And some stores and supermarkets sell strong plain [all-purpose] or baker's white flour which is particularly good for bread-making.

You can mix several different kinds of flour together. For example, you can make a good loaf of pale brown bread if you use a mixture of 4 ounces [1 cup] of 100 percent wholemeal flour and 12 ounces [3 cups] of ordinary soft household flour. Even better bread is produced if you use 85 percent or 90 percent wholemeal flour with strong plain or baker's white flour in the same proportions.

When making bread, it is best if the temperature of the flour is the same as that of the room and of the liquid used in the recipe. If the flour is too cold, you can warm it in the oven.

Yeast

The most important thing to remember about yeast is that it is a living cell which must be provided with a 'friendly' environment if it is to do its job properly.

Yeast is a very tiny fungus which grows by sending off buds to form new plants, and by forming spores which may also become new plants. As yeast grows it gives off carbon dioxide gas. This gas, when the yeast is mixed into the dough, causes the elastic cell walls of the gluten in the flour to expand—the phenomenon of the dough rising.

The yeast also gives off alcohol which, if growth is allowed to continue too long, develops into acetic acid and causes the dough to become sour. The heat of baking, however, drives off the alcohol.

Controversy still rages over fresh yeast versus dried yeast. Fresh bakers' yeast or compressed yeast (*not* brewers' yeast) is sold by health food shops and by some bakers and supermarkets. Because the plants in fresh yeast are active and alive it is highly perishable and can be kept only for four to five days in an airtight container in the refrigerator. Fresh yeast should feel cool and like putty to touch. It should be grey in colour and practically odourless. When you use it, it should break with a clean edge and crumble easily. Do not use yeast that is

1 In a large warmed bowl, make a well in the flour, salt and sugar. Pour in the liquid ingredients.

2 Using your hands, or a spatula, mix the ingredients together until all the flour is incorporated.

3 On a floured surface, knead the dough for about 10 minutes, or until it feels smooth and elastic.

dry or sour-smelling or has dark streaks.

Dried yeast in granule form (activated dried yeast) will keep for 6 months in a cool place because the plants are inert and will not become active until they are mixed with a warm liquid.

The quantity of yeast given in all our bread recipes is for fresh yeast. If you prefer to use dried yeast, the conversion is quite simple—half the quantity. In other words, use 1 ounce of fresh yeast or $\frac{1}{2}$ ounce of dried yeast. As a guide, use $\frac{1}{2}$ ounce of fresh yeast for 1 to $1\frac{1}{2}$ pounds of flour and 1 ounce of fresh yeast for 3 pounds of flour.

Yeast is destroyed by extreme heat—over 110°F. If you add hot water to yeast, or try to speed up the rising process by leaving the dough in a very hot place, the yeast will be killed. You can use cold water to dissolve the yeast and leave the dough to rise in the refrigerator overnight (this prolongs the rising process), but the yeast will develop most satisfactorily if the room temperature, the temperature of the flour and the temperature of the liquid are all between 75°F and 85°F.

Sugar

Sugar provides food for the yeast which helps it to grow and also adds flavour to the bread. Sugar also plays a part in browning the crust. If there is not very much sugar in the dough, the yeast will use it all in making carbon dioxide and alcohol, and the baked bread will not be golden brown.

Too much sugar, however, retards the yeast's activity and the dough will take longer to rise.

Liquid

The moisture in the dough is supplied by water or milk or a mixture of the two, and may be cold when it is added. The ideal temperature, however, is lukewarm (80°F to 85°F). Test the milk on the inside of your wrist.

Milk should be scalded (brought to just under the boiling point) and then cooled to lukewarm before it is added to the flour. This scalding destroys certain bacteria in the milk which could cause the dough to sour. It also makes the dough easier to handle.

Salt

Salt should never be mixed directly with the yeast because it slows down the fermentation process. But a sufficient amount of salt must be added to the dough or the bread will have a very uninteresting flavour.

Eggs and butter or oil

Eggs and butter or oil are variables. When eggs are added to the dough, as in sweet breads or French brioches, the finished bread is richer and more yellow. Butter or oil increase the volume of the baked bread because the gluten network of the dough is lubricated so that it expands more smoothly and easily. Butter or oil also improve the flavour and keeping qualities of the bread.

TECHNIQUES

Dissolving the Yeast

Crumble the yeast into a small bowl. Using a fork cream a small amount of sugar with the yeast and add a little lukewarm water. Mix to a paste and set aside in a warm, draught-free place to ferment. At the end of 15 to 20 minutes the yeast will be puffed up and frothy.

An alternative method is to add the yeast paste to a quarter of the specified amount of flour and mix it to a soft dough. Cut a cross in the top of this yeast ball with a knife and set it aside in a warm, draught-free place for 20 to 30 minutes to ferment. At the end of this time the yeast ball will be doubled in size.

If you are using dried yeast, dissolve a small quantity of sugar in lukewarm water in a small bowl or teacup and sprinkle on the yeast. Leave it for 10

minutes to allow the yeast cells to separate, swell and become active.

The yeast is now ready to begin its work as soon as it is added to the dough.

Mixing the Dough

Put the dry ingredients, the flour, salt and sugar, in a large warmed bowl. Make a well in the centre and into this pour the liquid ingredients, the dissolved yeast, milk and/or water, butter melted in the milk, or oil. Then, using your fingers or a spatula, gradually draw the dry ingredients into the liquids and continue mixing until all the flour is incorporated and the dough comes away from the sides of the bowl. If the dough is too soft and wet, more flour may be worked in.

Kneading

Turn the dough out of the bowl on to a floured board or marble slab to knead. This will thoroughly mix the flour with the liquid. The kneaded dough will hold in the gas bubbles manufactured by the yeast.

Fold the dough over on to itself towards you and then press it down away from yourself with the heels of your hands. Turn the dough slightly and fold and press it again. Continue kneading for about 10 minutes until the dough feels smooth and elastic. Dough made with hard-wheat flours requires a little more kneading than dough made with soft flour.

If the dough feels sticky while you are kneading, you may work in a little more flour, but be careful not to add too much or the dough will become stiff.

Rising

Shape the kneaded dough into a ball and place it in a lightly greased bowl. Sprinkle the surface of the dough with a little flour and cover the bowl with a damp cloth. The flour will prevent the dough from sticking to the cloth as it rises and

4 *Leave it in a warm place for 1 to 1½ hours, or until the dough has almost doubled in bulk. Remove the cover.*

5 *When the dough has risen, punch it to break up the air pockets, and fold the edges to the centre.*

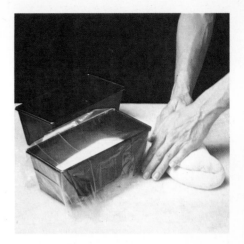

6 *Shape the dough into pieces and press them into greased loaf tins. Leave the dough to rise again.*

the cloth is dampened to increase the humidity. Do not cover the bowl tightly because to grow the yeast needs air as well as moisture, warmth and food. Place the bowl in a warm, draught-free place until the dough has almost doubled in bulk.

If your kitchen is cold you may want to place the bowl on top of the stove with the oven on at cool 300°F (Gas Mark 2, 150°C).

Rising times vary greatly depending on temperature, the amount of yeast in the dough and the kind of flour used, but, generally speaking, 1 to 1½ hours is adequate. The longer the fermentation, the better-flavoured and better-textured the bread will be. However, the dough should not be left to rise in a warm place for too long or it will become tough. You can tell if this is happening because a crust will form on the top of the dough.

If you want to speed up the rising process, place the covered bowl on an oven rack over a pan of boiling water. But be sure that the bottom of the bowl is not too close to the water or the heat will kill the yeast.

To test if the dough has risen sufficiently, press two fingers deep into the dough and withdraw them quickly. If the indentation remains the dough has risen enough.

If you are preparing the dough the day before the bread is to be baked, you can prolong the rising process by putting the covered bowl in a cool place or in the refrigerator for 8 to 10 hours or overnight. When the dough is fully risen it will be lighter and more spongy than dough which has risen in a warm place. It will require more kneading the second time as well as a longer proving. This slow rising method will, however, produce an excellent bread which will keep well.

Second Kneading

Push your fist into the centre of the dough and fold the edges to the centre. This punching down breaks up the large gas pockets and makes available a new supply of oxygen for the yeast plants.

Turn the dough out of the bowl on to the floured work surface. Knead it thoroughly and vigorously for 2 to 3 minutes (a larger batch of dough requires a longer kneading). This second kneading is more important than the first because it temporarily checks the action of the yeast.

Use a sharp knife to cut the dough into the number of loaves you are baking. With your hands, shape these pieces into balls.

Proving

What you are proving is that the yeast is still active. To do this the balls of dough are put into the greased tins and pushed out slightly so that they are roughly the shape of the tins. The tins should be only about half full. Sprinkle the surfaces of the loaves with a little flour. Cover the tins with a damp cloth and return them to a warm place for 45 to 60 minutes. During this time the dough will rise to the tops of the tins.

The proving may be done on an oven rack over a pan of boiling water, but be careful not to place the bottoms of the tins too close to the hot water.

If you want your bread to have a shiny crust, instead of sprinkling the dough with flour, just before baking brush the tops of the loaves with a mixture of beaten egg and milk.

A country-style finish can be produced by making a criss-cross gash in the top of the dough with a heated, sharp knife or kitchen scissors.

Baking

The bread must always be started in a hot oven so the oven should be preheated

to the correct temperature before the dough is put in to bake. Baking stops the fermentation of the yeast and evaporates the alcohol.

Place the tins in the centre of the oven and bake for 15 minutes. In this initial stage the loaf rises dramatically. This is caused by the leavening gas expanding rapidly and the gluten cells stretching to accommodate it.

Transfer the tins to a lower shelf and reduce the oven heat. The gluten cells will gradually be set by the heat, and after 25 to 30 minutes the bread should be done, having shrunk slightly in the tins.

To increase the crustiness of the loaves, brush the tops of the loaves with lightly beaten egg white or cold water 10 minutes before the end of the baking time. For a soft crust, brush the tops with melted butter 10 minutes before the baking time is completed.

Remove the tins from the oven and turn the bread out, upside-down, on to a wire rack. Rap the bottoms of the loaves with your knuckles. If they sound hollow, like a drum, the bread is cooked. If they feel soft, return them, upside-down, to the oven with the heat reduced and bake for a further 10 to 15 minutes.

A shiny, glazed crust, characteristic of French and Vienna bread or rolls, can be obtained by placing a flat pan of boiling water in the bottom of the oven just before the bread is put in and leaving the tin in the oven throughout the baking. The steam from the water forms a coating of moisture on the surface of the dough which gives it time to expand and develop a crust.

Cooling

Bread should be cooled on a wire rack so that the air can circulate around it and prevent moisture from spoiling the crispness of the crust.

American White Bread

☆   ①   ✗ ✗ ✗

This is a smooth-textured, pleasant-tasting milk bread. It has a shiny, golden brown crust and is excellent for sandwiches. This dough recipe can also be used successfully for fruit or nut loaves. For a fruit loaf, during the second kneading add either 5 ounces [1 cup] of raisins or dates, for a nut loaf, 5 ounces [1 cup] of chopped walnuts, hazelnuts or almonds. For a fruit and nut loaf, add 5 ounces [1 cup] of dried fruit and 3 ounces [¾ cup] of chopped walnuts, hazelnuts or almonds.

ONE 1-POUND LOAF

2 oz. [¼ cup] plus ½ teaspoon butter
½ oz. yeast
1 tablespoon plus 1 teaspoon sugar
3 teaspoons lukewarm water
10 fl. oz. [1¼ cups] milk
1 lb. [4 cups] flour
1 teaspoon salt
GLAZE
1 egg lightly beaten with 1
   tablespoon milk

Grease the loaf tin with the ½ teaspoon of butter and set aside.

Crumble the yeast into a small bowl and mash in the 1 teaspoon of sugar with a kitchen fork. Add the water and cream the water and yeast together to form a smooth paste. Set the bowl aside in a

A smooth milk bread with a golden brown crust, American White Bread is perfect for sandwiches.

---

warm, draught-free place for 15 to 20 minutes, or until the yeast has risen and is puffed up and frothy.

Pour the milk into a small saucepan, place it over moderately high heat and bring it to just below the boiling point. Then reduce the heat to low and add the remaining butter. When the butter has melted, remove the pan from the heat and allow the milk-and-butter mixture to cool to lukewarm.

Sift the flour, the remaining sugar and the salt into a large, warmed mixing bowl. Make a well in the centre of the flour mixture and pour in the yeast and the milk-and-butter mixture. Using your fingers or a spatula gradually draw the flour into the liquid. Continue mixing until all the flour is incorporated and the dough comes away from the sides of the bowl.

Turn the dough out on to a floured board or marble slab and knead for about 10 minutes, reflouring the surface if the dough becomes sticky. The dough should then be elastic and smooth.

Rinse, thoroughly dry and lightly grease the large mixing bowl. Shape the dough into a ball and return it to the

bowl. Dust the top of the dough with a little flour and cover the bowl with a clean, damp cloth. Set the bowl in a warm, draught-free place and leave it for 1 to 1½ hours, or until the dough has risen and has almost doubled in bulk.

Turn the risen dough out of the bowl on to a floured surface and knead for about 4 minutes. Roll and shape the dough into a loaf. Place the dough in the tin, cover with a damp cloth and return to a warm place for about 30 to 45 minutes, or until the dough has risen to the top of the tin.

Preheat the oven to very hot 475°F (Gas Mark 9, 240°C).

Using a pastry brush, paint the top of the loaf with the glaze. Place the tin in the centre of the oven and bake for 15 minutes. Then lower the temperature to hot 425°F (Gas Mark 7, 220°C), put the tin on a lower shelf in the oven and bake for another 25 to 30 minutes.

After removing the bread from the oven, tip the loaf out and rap the underside with your knuckles. If the bread sounds hollow, like a drum, it is cooked. If the bread does not sound hollow, lower the oven temperature to fairly hot 375°F (Gas Mark 5, 190°C), return the loaf, upside-down, to the oven and bake for a further 10 minutes.

Cool the loaf on a wire rack.

Simple and inexpensive to make, white Household Bread is the ideal loaf for beginner bread-makers.

Household Bread

  ①

Simple and economical to make, Household Bread is ordinary white bread, the type most often seen in shops. But like anything home-made, it certainly looks and tastes better. This recipe makes enough dough to fill four 1 pound loaf tins, but it is more interesting to bake the bread in different containers, or shape the dough into individual braids, rolls, long French-style loaves or round Italian-style loaves.

FOUR 1-POUND LOAVES

2 teaspoons butter
1 oz. yeast
1 tablespoon plus 1 teaspoon sugar
1½ pints [3¾ cups] plus 4 teaspoons lukewarm water
3 lb. [12 cups] flour
1 tablespoon salt

Grease the 4 tins with the butter.

Crumble the yeast into a small bowl and mash in 1 teaspoon of sugar with a kitchen fork. Add 4 teaspoons of water and cream the water and yeast together to form a smooth paste. Set the bowl aside in a warm, draught-free place for 15 to 20 minutes, or until the yeast has risen and is puffed up and frothy.

Put the flour, the remaining sugar and the salt into a warmed, large mixing bowl. Make a well in the centre of the flour mixture and pour in the yeast and the remaining lukewarm water. Using your hands or a spatula gradually draw the flour into the liquid. Continue mixing until all the flour is incorporated and the dough comes away from the sides of the bowl.

Turn the dough out on to a floured board or marble slab and knead for about 10 minutes, reflouring the surface if the dough becomes sticky. The dough should then be elastic and smooth.

Rinse, thoroughly dry and lightly grease the large mixing bowl. Shape the dough into a ball and return it to the bowl. Dust the top of the dough with a little flour and cover the bowl with a clean, damp cloth. Set the bowl in a warm, draught-free place and leave it for 1 to 1½ hours, or until the dough has risen and has almost doubled in bulk.

Turn the risen dough out of the bowl on to a floured surface and knead for about 8 to 10 minutes. Using a sharp knife, cut the dough into four pieces and roll and shape each piece into a loaf. Place the loaves in the tins, cover with a damp cloth and return to a warm place for about 30 to 45 minutes, or until the

This Quick Bread can be made when you're short of time since it requires only one rising and little kneading.

dough has risen to the top of the tins.

Preheat the oven to very hot 475°F (Gas Mark 9, 240°C).

Place the tins in the centre of the oven and bake for 15 minutes. Then lower the temperature to hot 425°F (Gas Mark 7, 220°C), put the bread on a lower shelf in the oven and bake for another 25 to 30 minutes.

After removing the bread from the oven, tip the loaves out of the tins and rap the undersides with your knuckles. If the bread sounds hollow, like a drum, it is cooked. If it does not sound hollow, lower the oven temperature to fairly hot 375°F (Gas Mark 5, 190°C), return the loaves, upside-down, to the oven and bake for a further 5 to 10 minutes.

Cool the loaves on a wire rack.

Quick Bread

 ①

This bread differs from other breads in that it requires only one rising and very little kneading. It has a slightly rough texture and does not keep as well as breads prepared in the usual way.

13

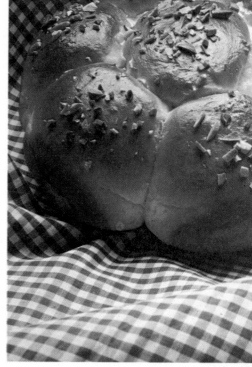

ONE 1-POUND LOAF

½ teaspoon butter
½ oz. yeast
1 teaspoon sugar
10 fl. oz. [1¼ cups] plus 3 teaspoons
   lukewarm water
12 oz. [3 cups] flour
4 oz. wholemeal flour [1 cup
   wholewheat flour]
1 teaspoon salt
1 tablespoon cracked wheat

Grease a loaf tin with the butter and
set aside.

Crumble the yeast into a small bowl
and mash in the sugar with a kitchen fork.
Add 3 teaspoons of water and cream the
water and yeast together to form a smooth
paste. Set the bowl aside in a warm,
draught-free place for 15 to 20 minutes,
or until the yeast has risen and is puffed
up and frothy.

Put the flour, the wholemeal [whole-
wheat] flour and the salt into a warmed,
large mixing bowl. Make a well in the
centre of the flour mixture and pour
in the yeast and the remaining water.
Using your fingers or a spatula gradually
draw the flour into the liquid. Continue
mixing until all the flour is incorporated
and the dough comes away from the
sides of the bowl.

Turn the dough out on to a floured
board or marble slab and knead it for

*Made from rye and wholewheat flours,
Swedish Rye Bread is flavourful and
light-textured.*

---

about 3 minutes.

Roll and shape the dough into a loaf
and place it in the tin. Cover the tin with
a clean damp cloth and set it aside in a
warm draught-free place for 1 to 1½
hours or until the dough has risen to the
top of the tin.

While the dough is rising, preheat the
oven to very hot 475°F (Gas Mark 9,
240°C).

Uncover the tin and sprinkle the top of
the dough with the tablespoon of cracked
wheat.

Place the tin in the centre of the oven
and bake for 15 minutes. Then lower
the temperature to hot 425°F (Gas
Mark 7, 220°C), put the tin on a lower
shelf in the oven and bake for another
25 to 30 minutes.

After removing the bread from the
oven, tip the loaf out and rap the underside with your knuckles. If the bread
sounds hollow, like a drum, it is cooked.
If it does not sound hollow, lower the
oven temperature to fairly hot 375°F
(Gas Mark 5, 190°C), return the loaf,
upside-down, to the oven and bake for a
further 5 to 10 minutes.

Cool the loaf on a wire rack.

Swedish Rye Bread

*The nutritious combination of rye and
wholewheat flours makes light-textured,
attractive brown bread. As with other
wholewheat breads, Swedish Rye, wrapped
in a clean dry cloth and stored in an
airtight container, keeps extremely well.*

TWO 1-POUND LOAVES

1 teaspoon butter
¾ oz. yeast
1½ tablespoons plus 1 teaspoon
   brown sugar
3 teaspoons lukewarm water
1 pint [2½ cups] milk
1 lb. [4 cups] stone-ground rye flour
1 lb. [4 cups] stone-ground
   wholewheat flour
1½ teaspoons salt
2 teaspoons caraway seeds
   (optional)

Grease two loaf tins with the butter and
set aside.

Crumble the yeast into a small bowl
and mash in 1 teaspoon of sugar with
a kitchen fork. Add 3 teaspoons of water
and cream the water and yeast together
to form a smooth paste. Set the bowl
aside in a warm draught-free place for 15
to 20 minutes, or until the yeast has risen
and is puffed up and frothy.

Pour the milk into a small saucepan,

Sweet Bread dough may be made into buns and sprinkled with nuts to be served for breakfast or with coffee.

place it over moderately high heat and bring it to just below boiling point. Remove the pan from the heat and allow the milk to cool to lukewarm.

Put the rye flour, the wholewheat flour and the salt into a warmed, large mixing bowl. Add the remaining sugar and mix the ingredients together well.

Make a well in the centre of the flour mixture and pour in the yeast and all the milk. Using your fingers or a spatula, gradually draw the flour into the liquid. Continue mixing until all the flour is incorporated and the dough comes away from the sides of the bowl.

Turn the dough out on to a floured board or marble slab and knead for about 10 minutes, reflouring the surface if the dough becomes sticky. The dough should then be elastic and smooth.

Rinse, thoroughly dry and lightly grease the large mixing bowl, shape the dough into a ball and return it to the bowl. Dust the top of the dough with a little flour and cover the bowl with a clean, damp cloth. Put the bowl in a warm, draught-free place for 1 to 1½ hours, or until the dough has risen and has almost doubled in bulk.

Turn the risen dough out of the bowl on to a floured surface and knead vigorously for about 4 minutes. Knead in the caraway seeds, if you are using them. Using a sharp knife, cut the dough into two pieces. Roll and shape each piece into a loaf. Place the loaves in the tins, cover with a damp cloth and return to a warm place for about 30 to 45 minutes, or until the dough has risen to the top of the tins.

Preheat the oven to very hot 475°F (Gas Mark 9, 240°C).

Place the tins in the centre of the oven and bake for 15 minutes. Then lower the temperature to hot 425°F (Gas Mark 7, 220°C). Put the bread on a lower shelf in the oven and bake for another 25 to 30 minutes.

After removing the bread from the oven, tip the loaves out and rap the undersides with your knuckles. If the bread sounds hollow, like a drum, it is cooked. If the bread does not sound hollow, lower the oven temperature to fairly hot 375°F (Gas Mark 5, 190°C), return the loaves, upside-down, to the oven, and bake for a further 10 minutes.

Cool the loaves on a wire rack.

Sweet Bread

This basic Sweet Bread recipe can be used successfully in many ways. The dough baked in loaf tins can be served as a plain sweet bread spread with butter or jam. Baked in a ring mould filled with fruit and nuts or iced and sprinkled with chopped nuts it makes an attractive coffee cake. Alternatively, it may be shaped into buns, baked on a baking sheet, and served as sweet rolls for breakfast or with tea. If you are making a sweet fruit loaf or buns, add approximately 5 ounces [1 cup] of mixed fruit and candied peel for each 1 pound of flour.

TWO 1-POUND LOAVES

4 oz. [½ cup] plus 1 teaspoon butter
½ oz. yeast
4 oz. [½ cup] plus ½ teaspoon sugar
3 teaspoons lukewarm water
8 fl. oz. [1 cup] milk
1½ lb. [6 cups] flour
1 teaspoon salt
2 eggs, lightly beaten
GLAZE
1 egg lightly beaten with
1 tablespoon milk

Grease the loaf tins with 1 teaspoon of butter.

Crumble the yeast into a small bowl and mash in ½ teaspoon of sugar with a kitchen fork. Add 3 teaspoons of

water and cream the water and yeast together to form a smooth paste. Set the bowl aside in a warm, draught-free place for about 15 to 20 minutes, or until the yeast mixture has risen and is puffed up and frothy.

Pour the milk into a small saucepan. Place it over moderately high heat and bring it to just below the boiling point. Reduce the heat to low and add the remaining butter. When the butter has melted, remove the pan from the heat and allow the milk-and-butter mixture to cool to lukewarm.

Sift the flour, remaining sugar and salt into a warmed, large mixing bowl. Make a well in the centre of the flour mixture and pour in the yeast, milk-and-butter mixture and the 2 eggs. Using your fingers, or a spatula, gradually draw the flour into the liquid. Continue mixing until all the flour is incorporated and the dough comes away from the sides of the bowl.

Turn the dough out on to a floured board or marble slab and knead for about 10 minutes, reflouring the surface if the dough becomes sticky. The dough should then be elastic and smooth.

Rinse, thoroughly dry and lightly grease the large mixing bowl. Shape the dough into a ball and return it to the bowl. Dust the top of the dough with a little flour and cover the bowl with a clean, damp cloth. Set the bowl in a warm, draught-free place and leave it for 1 to 1½ hours, or until the dough has risen and has almost doubled in bulk.

Turn the risen dough out of the bowl on to a floured surface and knead it for about 4 minutes. Using a sharp knife cut the dough into 2 pieces. Roll and shape each piece into a loaf. Place the dough in the tins, cover with a damp cloth and return to a warm place for about 30 to 45 minutes, or until the dough has risen to the top of the tins.

Preheat the oven to very hot 475°F (Gas Mark 9, 240°C).

Using a pastry brush, paint the tops of the loaves with the glaze. Place the tins in the centre of the oven and bake for 15 minutes. Then lower the temperature to hot 425°F (Gas Mark 7, 220°C), put the tins on a lower shelf in the oven and bake for another 25 to 30 minutes.

After removing the bread from the oven, tip the loaves out and rap the undersides with your knuckles. If the bread sounds hollow, like a drum, it is cooked. If it does not sound hollow, lower the oven temperature to fairly hot 375°F (Gas Mark 5, 190°C), return the loaves, upside-down, to the oven and bake for a further 5 to 10 minutes.

Cool the loaves on a wire rack.

ously for about 10 minutes. Using a sharp knife, cut the dough into four pieces. Roll and shape each piece into a loaf. Place the loaves in the tins. If you prefer a country-style loaf, use a heated, sharp knife or kitchen scissors to make a deep gash on the top of each loaf and then dust them with a little wholewheat flour. Cover the tins with a damp cloth and return to a warm place for 30 to 45 minutes, or until the dough has risen to the top of the tins.

Preheat the oven to very hot 475°F (Gas Mark 9, 240°C).

Place the tins in the centre of the oven and bake for 15 minutes. Then lower the oven temperature to hot 425°F (Gas Mark 7, 220°C), put the bread on a lower shelf in the oven and bake for another 25 to 30 minutes.

After removing the bread from the oven, tip the loaves out of the tins and rap the undersides with your knuckles. If the bread sounds hollow, like a drum, it is cooked. If the bread does not sound hollow, lower the oven temperature to fairly hot 375°F (Gas Mark 5, 190°C), return the loaves, upside-down, to the oven and bake for a further 10 minutes.

Cool the loaves on a wire rack.

Wholewheat Bread

Home-made wholewheat bread is far superior to any commercial brown bread. Although it is most delicious when freshly baked and spread with butter, honey or cheese, stored correctly the bread keeps extremely well and can be served up to a week after baking. For variation the loaves may be baked in well-greased flower pots, or shaped into cottage loaves on a baking sheet.

To make cheese bread, add 12 ounces of finely grated Cheddar or any hard cheese to the flour with the yeast mixture.

FOUR 1-POUND LOAVES

1½ teaspoons butter
1 oz. yeast
1 teaspoon brown sugar
1½ pints [3¾ cups] plus 4 teaspoons lukewarm water
3 lb. [12 cups] stone-ground wholewheat flour
1¼ tablespoon rock salt or 1 tablespoon table salt
2 tablespoons honey
1 tablespoon vegetable oil

Grease the 4 loaf tins with the butter.

Crumble the yeast into a small bowl and mash in the brown sugar with a kitchen fork. Add 4 teaspoons of water and cream the water, sugar and yeast together to form a smooth paste. Set the

For an attractive, unusual-shaped loaf, Wholewheat Bread can be baked in well-greased flower pots.

bowl aside in a warm, draught-free place for 15 to 20 minutes, or until the yeast has risen and is puffed up and frothy.

Put the flour and salt into a warmed, large mixing bowl. Make a well in the centre of the flour mixture and pour in the yeast mixture, the honey, the remaining lukewarm water and the oil. Using your fingers, or a spatula, gradually draw the flour into the liquid. Continue mixing until all the flour is incorporated and the dough comes away from the sides of the bowl.

Turn the dough out on to a floured board or marble slab and knead for about 10 minutes, reflouring the surface if the dough becomes sticky. The dough should then be elastic and smooth.

Rinse, thoroughly dry and lightly grease the large mixing bowl. Shape the dough into a ball and return it to the bowl. Dust the top of the dough with a little flour and cover the bowl with a clean, damp cloth. Set the bowl in a warm, draught-free place and leave it for 1 to 1½ hours, or until the dough has risen and has almost doubled in bulk.

Turn the risen dough out of the bowl on to a floured surface and knead vigor-

Corn

Generally speaking, corn means any grain, the seed of any cereal plant. In the United States it refers to maize, in England it usually means wheat and in Scotland, oats.

In culinary terms it always means maize or Indian corn.

Native to North and South America and cultivated as long ago as 2,000 B.C., maize was introduced into Europe by Columbus in the fifteenth century. Within a hundred years it had spread to Africa, India and China.

There are many varieties of maize, but the three which are of culinary interest are: dent corn, used mainly in the preparation of various cornflours, pop corn, so called because when heated the moisture in the kernels expands causing them to explode, Indian or sweet corn, used almost exclusively for human consumption as a vegetable (also known as green corn because it is picked and cooked before it is ripe). Sweet corn is delicious boiled or roasted and eaten hot with butter. It is also available canned and frozen.

Corn Bread

In the United States, Corn Bread is served

hot with butter and honey as an accompaniment to fried chicken. It is also delicious for tea, spread with butter and jam.

8-INCH SQUARE CORN BREAD

1 teaspoon butter
5½ oz. [1 cup] yellow corn meal
4 oz. [1 cup] flour
2 teaspoons baking powder
1 teaspoon salt
2 oz. [¼ cup] vegetable fat
8 fl. oz. [1 cup] milk
1 egg

Preheat the oven to fairly hot 400°F (Gas Mark 6, 200°C).

Using the teaspoon of butter, lightly grease an 8-inch baking tin. Sift the corn meal, flour, baking powder and salt into a medium-sized mixing bowl. Add the vegetable fat and with a table knife cut the fat into the flour until it is in small pieces. With your fingertips, rub the fat into the flour until the mixture resembles fine breadcrumbs.

In a small mixing bowl, beat the milk and egg together with a fork.

Using a wooden spoon, stir the egg-and-milk mixture into the flour mixture until the ingredients are well blended.

Turn the mixture into the greased baking tin. Place the tin in the oven and bake for 25 minutes, or until a skewer inserted into the centre of the bread comes out clean.

Remove the tin from the oven. Cut the corn bread into 2-inch squares and lift them out of the tin on to a serving plate. Serve at once.

Rich Corn Meal Bread

A deliciously rich American bread, Rich Corn Meal Bread is best served warm with lots of butter and jam.

ONE 8-INCH CORN BREAD

4 oz. [½ cup] plus 1 teaspoon butter, melted
6 oz. [1½ cups] flour
4 teaspoons baking powder
1 teaspoon salt
10 oz. [2 cups] yellow corn meal
1 teaspoon sugar
4 eggs, lightly beaten
8 fl. oz. [1 cup] milk
2 fl. oz. single cream [¼ cup light cream]

Preheat the oven to fairly hot 400°F (Gas Mark 6, 200°C).

Using the teaspoon of butter, lightly grease an 8-inch square baking tin. Set aside.

Sift the flour, baking powder and salt into a large mixing bowl. Stir in the corn meal and sugar.

Cut the remaining butter into the flour with a table knife. With your fingertips, rub the fat into the flour mixture until the mixture resembles coarse breadcrumbs.

In a small mixing bowl, beat the eggs and milk together with a fork.

Using a wooden spoon, stir the egg mixture into the flour mixture until the ingredients are well blended. Stir the cream into the mixture to form a thick paste.

Spoon the batter into the baking tin and smooth the top with a knife. Place the tin in the oven and bake for 25 to 35 minutes or until a skewer inserted into the centre of the bread comes out clean.

Remove the tin from the oven and allow it to cool for 5 minutes. Cut the corn bread into 2-inch squares and lift them out of the tin on to a serving plate. Serve warm.

Oat

One of the earliest cereals cultivated by man, the oat is used both as a food for man, and a fodder for animals.

As food for man, oats are ground into OATMEAL, or flattened into rolled oats — a process which involves heating the grains while passing them through rollers.

All types of oats contain protein, fat, carbohydrates, iron, calcium and Vitamin B. Because of the fat contents, oats do not keep well, so they should be bought in small quantities and stored in an airtight tin.

Oats contain very little gluten, so they are not suitable for making bread, unless they are mixed with another cereal.

Oat Bread

A delicious, coarse bread made with rolled oats, Oat Bread makes nutritious sandwiches with cheese or cold meat.

TWO 1-POUND LOAVES

½ oz. fresh yeast
½ teaspoon sugar
3 tablespoons lukewarm water
1 pint [2½ cups] milk
2 oz. [⅓ cup] soft brown sugar

Oat Bread, spread with plenty of butter, is delicious eaten on its own, or with cheese.

3 oz. [⅜ cup] butter, melted
1½ lb. [6 cups] flour
1 teaspoon salt
12 oz. [3 cups] rolled oats
2 teaspoons vegetable oil

Crumble the yeast into a small bowl and mash in the sugar with a kitchen fork. Add the water and cream the yeast and water together. Set the bowl aside in a warm, draught-free place for 15 to 20 minutes or until the yeast mixture is puffed up and frothy.

Meanwhile, in medium-sized saucepan, scald the milk over moderate heat (bring to just under boiling point). Stir in the brown sugar and 2 ounces [¼ cup] of the butter. Continue to stir until the sugar has dissolved. Remove the pan from the heat and set aside to cool to lukewarm.

Sift the flour and salt into a warmed, large mixing bowl. Stir in the oats. Make a well in the centre and pour in the yeast and milk mixtures. Using your fingers or a spatula, gradually draw the flour mixture into the liquids. Continue mixing until all the flour mixture is incorporated and the dough comes away from the sides of the bowl.

Turn the dough out on to a lightly floured board or marble slab and knead it for 10 minutes, reflouring the surface if the dough becomes sticky. The dough should be elastic and smooth.

Rinse, thoroughly dry and lightly grease the large mixing bowl. Shape the dough into a ball and return it to the bowl. Cover the bowl with a clean damp cloth and set it in a warm, draught-free place. Leave it for 1¾ to 2 hours or until the dough has risen and almost doubled in bulk.

Using a pastry brush, grease two 1-pound loaf tins with the oil. Set aside.

Turn the risen dough out of the bowl on to a floured surface and knead it for 4 minutes. Divide the dough into two and shape into loaves. Place the loaves in the prepared tins and brush with the remaining melted butter.

Return the tins to a warm draught-free place for about 1 hour or until the dough has almost doubled in bulk and risen to the tops of the tins.

Preheat the oven to hot 425°F (Gas Mark 7, 220°C).

Place the tins in the centre of the oven and bake for 15 minutes. Reduce the oven temperature to fairly hot 375°F (Gas Mark 5, 190°C), put the tins on a lower shelf in the oven and continue baking for 25 minutes.

Remove the tins from the oven. Tip the loaves out of the tins and rap the undersides with your knuckles. If the bread sounds hollow, like a drum, it is cooked.

If not, reduce the oven temperature to warm 325°F (Gas Mark 3, 170°C), return the loaves to the oven, upside-down, and bake for a further 5 minutes.

Cool the loaves on a wire rack before serving.

Oat and Caraway Bread

A quick, easy-to-prepare bread, Oat and Caraway Bread is delicious thickly sliced and spread with butter.

ONE 1-POUND LOAF

1 oz. [2 tablespoons] plus 1 teaspoon butter, melted
10 oz. [2½ cups] wholewheat flour
1 teaspoon baking powder
½ teaspoon bicarbonate of soda [baking soda]
½ teaspoon salt
2 oz. [½ cup] rolled oats
2 oz. [⅔ cup] wheat germ
1 teaspoon caraway seeds
5 fl. oz. [⅝ cup] sour cream
2 eggs, lightly beaten
3 oz. [½ cup] soft brown sugar

Preheat the oven to moderate 350°F (Gas Mark 4, 180°C). Using the teaspoon of butter, lightly grease a 1-pound loaf tin and set aside.

Put the flour, baking powder, soda and salt into a large mixing bowl. Add the oats, wheat germ and caraway seeds and stir well to mix. Set aside.

In a small mixing bowl, combine the sour cream, eggs and sugar, beating well to blend. Make a well in the centre of the flour mixture and pour in the cream and egg mixture and the remaining melted butter. Using your fingers or a spatula, gradually draw the flour mixture into the liquids. Continue mixing until all the flour is incorporated and a soft dough is formed.

Turn the dough into the prepared tin and place the tin in the oven. Bake the bread for 40 to 50 minutes or until the top is golden brown.

Remove the tin from the oven and remove the loaf from the tin. Set aside on a wire rack to cool completely before serving.

Barley

A cultivated cereal as old as the earliest beginning of agriculture, barley is grown over a wider range of climate than any other grain. One of the five staple grains used for human consumption and malting, barley is most important as a livestock feed.

Barley is believed to have been used by prehistoric man for making beer.

Today, more than 10 per cent of the world crop is used for this purpose.

When the husk is removed barley is called pot barley, scotch barley or hulled barley and is used in the preparation of stews, soups and haggis. Husked barley, steamed, rounded and polished in a mill, is known as pearl barley and is used to thicken soups and stews. Pearl barley ground into a fine flour, is called patent barley.

When barley is ground coarsely to make a wholemeal flour it is called barley meal and is used to make porridge and gruel. It is also used in the preparation of some kinds of bread. Pressed and flattened barley grains are called barley flakes and are used in making milk puddings and gruel.

Barley Bread

Barley Bread, which has a subtle, delicate flavour, is close-textured and retains its freshness for a number of days. Dried yeast is used in this recipe, but fresh yeast may be used instead if it is easily available (use double the quantity for fresh yeast).

ONE 9-INCH LOAF

2 tablespoons plus 1 teaspoon butter
2 teaspoons brown sugar
16 fl. oz. [2 cups] lukewarm water
1 level tablespoon dried yeast
1½ lb. barley meal, warmed
1 tablespoon salt

Lightly grease a 9¼-inch loaf tin with 1 teaspoon butter.

In a small mixing bowl, dissolve 1 teaspoon of the sugar in 5 fluid ounces of warm water. Sprinkle the yeast on top and whisk it well with a fork to mix. Put the bowl in a warm place to stand for 20 minutes or until the yeast becomes frothy.

Sift the barley meal, salt and the remaining sugar into a large, warmed mixing bowl. With your fingertips, rub in the 2 tablespoons of butter.

Make a well in the centre of the dry mixture and pour in the frothy yeast liquid and the remaining warm water. Mix quickly and lightly with your hands until the mixture forms a dough. Turn the dough on to a floured board and knead well for 5 minutes. Place the dough in a greased bowl and cover with a clean cloth, or place in a polythene bag, and leave in a warm place for 1 hour or until the dough doubles in size.

Preheat the oven to fairly hot 400°F (Gas Mark 6, 200°C).

Turn the risen dough on to a floured

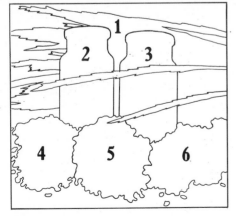

Barley

1 Spikes of barley	*2 Patent barley*
3 Barley meal	*4 Pot barley*
5 Flaked barley	*6 Pearl barley*

board and knead again for 5 minutes. Put the dough into the loaf tin, cover it with the cloth, or put it into the polythene bag, and leave it in a warm place for 20 minutes.

Place the loaf in the centre of the oven and bake for 1 hour. To test the loaf, rap the underside with your knuckles. If it sounds hollow it is done.

When the loaf is done, turn it out of the tin and cool on a rack.

Millet

Millet is a highly nutritious cereal, known from ancient times, which is grown in tropical and temperate climates. The species grown in the tropics forms part of the staple diet of the peoples living in the dry, drought-prone areas of Africa and Asia.

Sorghum, finger and bulrush millet are those most widely grown. The cereal is pounded and eaten in the form of a porridge and sorghum is also used for making beer.

Millet Bread

This is an unusual pancake-type bread, adapted from a North African recipe, where millet is an important staple food. Serve Millet Bread with butter and honey or jam. Alternatively, serve it with a savoury spread such as liver pâté.

8 SERVINGS

½ oz. fresh yeast
¼ teaspoon sugar
2 tablespoons lukewarm milk
8 oz. [2 cups] millet flour
½ teaspoon salt
6 fl. oz. [¾ cup] lukewarm water
1 oz. [2 tablespoons] vegetable fat, melted

Crumble the yeast into a small bowl and mash in the sugar with a kitchen fork. Add the milk and cream the milk and yeast together. Set the bowl aside in a warm, draught-free place for 15 to 20 minutes or until the yeast mixture is puffed up and frothy.

Sift the flour and salt into a warmed, medium-sized mixing bowl. Make a well in the centre and pour in the yeast mixture. Pour in the water, stirring constantly with a wooden spoon to form a thin, smooth batter. Beat the batter for 1 minute. Cover the bowl with a clean damp cloth and set it aside in a warm, draught-free place. Leave it for 45 minutes or until it has increased in bulk and is very frothy.

Heat a girdle or heavy-based frying-pan over low heat for 3 minutes or until it is hot. Using a pastry brush, coat the girdle or pan with a little of the melted vegetable fat. Pour about one-eighth of the batter on to the girdle or pan and cook it for 4 minutes or until the top of the mixture has set. Turn the bread over and cook on the other side for 4 minutes or until it is deep golden brown. Remove the bread from the girdle or pan and keep warm while you cook the remaining batter in the same way.

Serve hot.

Rye

Rye is a hardy cereal grass cultivated for its grain, which grows in Russia and other parts of northern Europe. It will grow in poor soil and has a high resistance to bad weather conditions.

The brown grain is milled into several grades of flour, ranging from fine to wholemeal. Fine rye flour is comparatively low in calories and is the one usually used in making crispbreads. Heavier wholemeal flour is used in making black bread.

Rye flour has a fairly high protein and calcium content and, when cooked, will keep much longer than bread or cakes made with ordinary white flour.

In breadmaking, rye flour is usually combined with some other flour, since its gluten content is low and, if used on its own, it produces a heavy, close-textured bread.

Some types of alcohol, such as WHISKY

and KVASS, are distilled from rye, and the plant left after the grain has been separated is sometimes used for animal fodder.

Rye Bread

Rye Bread looks as good as it tastes — and it's nutritious, too! Serve sliced, with plenty of butter. Or try it with cheese or garlic sausage for a special snack.

SIX 12-OUNCE LOAVES

1 oz. fresh yeast
1 teaspoon sugar
1½ pints [3¾ cups] plus 4 tablespoons lukewarm water
2 lb. [8 cups] rye flour
1 lb. [4 cups] strong white flour
1½ tablespoons salt
1 tablespoon soft brown sugar
1½ tablespoons vegetable oil
1 tablespoon butter
GLAZE
1 egg white lightly beaten with 1 tablespoon water

Crumble the yeast into a small bowl and mash in the sugar with a kitchen fork. Add the 4 tablespoons of lukewarm water and cream the water and yeast together to form a smooth paste. Set the bowl aside in a warm draught-free place for 15 to 20 minutes or until the yeast is puffed up and frothy.

Put the rye flour, white flour and salt into a very large mixing bowl. Add the soft brown sugar and mix the ingredients together well. Make a well in the centre of the flour mixture and pour in the yeast mixture, the oil and enough of the remaining water to make the dough pliable. Using your fingers or a spatula, gradually draw the flour mixture into the liquids. Continue mixing until all the flour is incorporated and the dough comes away from the sides of the bowl.

Turn the dough out on to a lightly floured board or marble slab and knead it for 10 minutes, reflouring the surface if the dough becomes sticky. The dough should be elastic and smooth.

Rinse, thoroughly dry and lightly grease the mixing bowl. Shape the dough into a ball and return it to the bowl. Cover the bowl with a clean damp cloth and set it in a warm, draught-free place for 2 hours or until the dough has risen and has almost doubled in bulk.

Using the butter, grease two very large baking sheets and set aside.

Turn the dough out of the bowl on to a floured surface and knead it for a further 10 minutes. Using a sharp knife, cut the dough into 6 equal pieces, then shape

Chewy and nutritious, Rye Bread is super served with lots of butter and cheese.

each piece into a ball. Place 3 of the balls on each baking sheet. Cover the baking sheets with 2 damp cloths and set aside for 30 to 40 minutes or until the balls have risen and almost doubled in bulk.

Meanwhile, preheat the oven to fairly hot 375°F (Gas Mark 5, 190°C).

Place the baking sheets in the centre of the oven and bake for 20 minutes. Remove the baking sheets from the oven and, using a pastry brush, brush the tops of the loaves with half of the glaze. Return the baking sheets to the oven and bake for a further 20 minutes. Remove the baking sheets from the oven and, with the pastry brush, brush the loaves again with the remaining glaze. Return the baking sheets to the oven and bake for a further 20 to 25 minutes or until the loaves are rich, golden brown in colour and the under-sides of the loaves sound hollow when rapped with your knuckles.

If the loaves do not sound hollow, lower the oven temperature to warm 325°F (Gas Mark 3, 170°C), return the loaves, upside-down, to the oven and bake for a further 5 minutes.

Cool the loaves on a wire rack.

Quick Bread II

This nourishing soda bread is very quick and easy to prepare. Serve it in chunks while still warm, accompanied by lots of unsalted butter.

ONE 1¼-POUND LOAF

1 teaspoon butter
1 lb. wholemeal flour [4 cups wholewheat flour]
4 oz. [1 cup] flour, sifted
1 teaspoon salt
1¼ teaspoon bicarbonate of soda [baking soda]
1 teaspoon cream of tartar
10 fl. oz. [1¼ cups] milk
2 tablespoons treacle or molasses
2 teaspoons wheat germ

Preheat the oven to hot 425°F (Gas Mark 7, 220°C).

Grease a large baking sheet with the butter and set aside.

Put the wholemeal [wholewheat] flour, sifted flour, salt, soda and cream of tartar into a large mixing bowl. With a wooden spoon, gradually stir in the milk, then the treacle or molasses to form a soft dough. If necessary, add a little more milk to obtain the correct consistency.

21

Turn the dough out on to a floured board and knead it for 1 minute. Shape the dough into a round shape, approximately 1½-inches thick and 6-inches in diameter.

Put the loaf on the baking sheet and sprinkle over the wheat germ. With a sharp knife, cut a deep cross on top of the loaf. Place the baking sheet in the oven and bake the loaf for 40 to 45 minutes or until the top is golden brown and the underside sounds hollow, like a drum, when it is rapped with your knuckles.

Remove the loaf from the oven. Transfer the loaf to a wire rack and allow it to cool slightly. Serve warm.

Egg Bread

This beautifully light Egg Bread, or Challah, is plaited [braided] and sprinkled with poppy seeds. It is traditionally baked for Hebrew Sabbaths and festivals. For Rosh Hashana the same bread is shaped into round loaves.

ONE 2-POUND LOAF

½ oz. fresh yeast
1½ tablespoons sugar
6 fl. oz. [¾ cup] milk, lukewarm
1 lb. [4 cups] flour
1½ teaspoons salt
2 eggs, beaten
1 tablespoon vegetable oil
½ teaspoon butter
GLAZE
1 egg, yolk, beaten with 1 tablespoon cold water
2 tablespoons poppy seeds

Crumble the yeast into a small bowl and mash in ½ teaspoon of the sugar with a fork. Add 2 teaspoons of the warm milk and cream the milk and yeast together to form a smooth paste. Cover the bowl with a clean cloth and set it aside in a warm, draught-free place for 15 to 20 minutes, or until the yeast mixture has risen and is puffed up and frothy.

Sift the flour, remaining sugar and the salt into a large, warmed mixing bowl. Make a well in the centre of the flour mixture and pour in the yeast mixture. Add the remaining milk, eggs and oil and using your fingers or a spatula, gradually draw the flour into the liquid. Continue mixing until all the flour is incorporated and the dough comes away from the sides of the bowl.

Cover the bowl with a clean damp cloth. Set the bowl in a warm, draught-free place and leave it for 1½ to 2 hours, or until the dough has risen and has almost doubled in bulk.

Grease a large baking sheet with the butter.

Turn the risen dough out of the bowl on to a lightly floured surface and knead it for about 5 to 8 minutes. Divide the dough into three ropes, each about 12-inches long. Fasten the ropes together at one end and loosely plait [braid] the three pieces together, fastening again at the end.

Preheat the oven to hot 425°F (Gas Mark 7, 220°C).

Place the loaf on the greased baking sheet and cover it again with a clean cloth. Set it aside in a warm place for 2 to 2½ hours, or until the loaf has risen and expanded across the baking sheet.

With a pastry brush, paint the top of the loaf with the egg yolk glaze and sprinkle the poppy seeds over the top. Place the baking sheet in the centre of the oven and bake for 10 minutes. Then reduce the temperature to fairly hot 375°F (Gas Mark 5, 190°C) and bake for a further 25 to 30 minutes or until the loaf is deep golden brown.

After removing the bread from the oven, tip the loaf off the baking sheet and rap the underside with your knuckles. If the bread sounds hollow, like a drum, it is cooked. If it does not sound hollow, return it to the oven for a further 5 to 10 minutes.

Cool the loaf on a wire rack.

Norwegian Soda Bread

Quick and easy to make, Norwegian Soda Bread should be eaten with plenty of butter and is excellent with soup.

TWO 6-INCH LOAVES

2 oz. [¼ cup] plus 1 teaspoon unsalted butter, melted
8 oz. [2 cups] rye flour
8 oz. [2 cups] wholewheat flour
1 teaspoon baking powder
1½ teaspoons bicarbonate of soda [baking soda]

1 teaspoon salt
1 tablespoon soft brown sugar
8 fl. oz. [1 cup] buttermilk
1 egg, lightly beaten

Preheat the oven to hot 425°F (Gas Mark 7, 220°C).

Grease a large baking sheet with the teaspoon of butter and set aside.

Sift the rye flour, wholewheat flour, baking powder, soda and salt into a large mixing bowl. Stir in the sugar.

In a medium-sized mixing bowl, mix together the remaining melted butter and the buttermilk. Make a well in the centre of the flour mixture and pour in the buttermilk mixture and the egg. Using your fingertips or a spatula, gradually draw the flour mixture into the liquids. Continue mixing until all the flour is incorporated and the dough comes away from the sides of the bowl.

Transfer the dough to a floured board and knead it lightly. Divide the dough in half and shape each piece into a flat round shape, approximately ½-inch thick.

Place the dough rounds on the baking sheet.

Place the baking sheet in the oven and bake for 20 to 25 minutes, or until the loaves are browned.

Remove the baking sheet from the oven. Allow the loaves to cool slightly and serve warm, or transfer them to a wire rack to cool completely.

Irish Soda Bread

This traditional Irish bread is surprisingly quick and easy to prepare. It should be served slightly warm with butter and jam for tea.

ONE 8-INCH LOAF

1 teaspoon butter
1 lb. [4 cups] flour
1 teaspoon bicarbonate of soda
[baking soda]
1 teaspoon salt
4 to 8 fl. oz. [½ cup to 1 cup] buttermilk

Preheat the oven to hot 425°F (Gas Mark 7, 220°C).

Grease a large baking sheet with the butter and set it aside.

Sift the flour, soda and salt into a large mixing bowl. With a wooden spoon, gradually beat in 4 fluid ounces [½ cup] of buttermilk. The dough should be smooth but firm. If necessary, add more buttermilk.

Transfer the dough to a floured board and shape it into a flat round loaf, approximately 1½-inches thick and 8-inches in diameter.

Place the loaf on the baking sheet. With a sharp knife, cut a deep cross on top of the loaf.

Place the loaf in the oven and bake for 30 to 35 minutes, or until the top is golden brown.

Remove the loaf from the oven and allow it to cool. Serve slightly warm.

Lvov Black Bread

An adaptation of an old Ukrainian recipe, Lvov Black Bread is both nutritious and delicious. Serve with lots of butter and a good, strong cheese.

ONE 1½-POUND LOAF

2 teaspoons vegetable oil
¾ oz. fresh yeast
½ teaspoon soft brown sugar
10 fl. oz. [1¼ cups] plus 2 tablespoons lukewarm water
2 tablespoons clear honey
3 tablespoons black treacle [molasses]
1 oz. [¼ cup] wheatgerm
6 oz. [1½ cups] flour
12 oz. [3 cups] rye flour
1½ teaspoons salt
1 teaspoon ground coriander
1 teaspoon ground cinnamon
2 oz. [¼ cup] butter, melted

With 1 teaspoon of the oil, grease a baking sheet. Set it aside.

Crumble the yeast into a small bowl and mash in the sugar with a fork. Add the 2 tablespoons of water and cream the water and yeast together to form a smooth paste. Set the bowl aside in a warm,

Much easier to make than other bread but just as delicious, Irish Soda Bread should be served still slightly warm, with butter and cheese or jam.

draught-free place for 15 to 20 minutes or until the yeast mixture is puffed up and frothy.

Meanwhile, put the honey, treacle [molasses] and wheatgerm in a medium-sized mixing bowl. Pour over the remaining water and stir to dissolve the wheatgerm. Set aside.

Sift the flour, rye flour, salt, coriander and cinnamon into a warmed large mixing bowl. Make a well in the centre and pour in the yeast mixture, wheatgerm mixture and the melted butter. Using your hands or a spatula, gradually draw the flour mixture into the liquids. Continue mixing

until all the flour is incorporated and the dough comes away from the sides of the bowl. If the dough is too dry, add more water.

Turn the dough out on to a lightly floured board or marble slab and knead it for 10 minutes, reflouring the surface if the dough becomes sticky. The dough should be elastic and smooth.

Rinse, thoroughly dry and lightly grease the large mixing bowl. Shape the dough into a ball and return it to the bowl. Cover the bowl with a clean, damp cloth and set it in a warm, draught-free place. Leave it for 1 to 1½ hours, or until the dough has risen and almost doubled in bulk.

Turn the risen dough out of the bowl on to a floured surface and knead it for

about 8 to 10 minutes. Roll and shape the dough into a high round loaf. Place the loaf on the baking sheet and return it to a warm place for about 30 to 45 minutes or until the dough has almost doubled in bulk again.

Preheat the oven to very hot 475°F (Gas Mark 9, 240°C).

With a pastry brush, lightly coat the top of the loaf with the remaining oil.

Place the baking sheet in the centre of the oven and bake for 15 minutes. Then lower the temperature to hot 425°F (Gas Mark 7, 220°C), put the baking sheet on a lower shelf in the oven and continue baking for 20 to 30 minutes, or until it is well browned.

After removing the bread from the oven, tip the loaf off the baking sheet and

Ukrainian Lvov Black Bread is delicious with butter and a strong cheese.

rap the underside with your knuckles. If the bread sounds hollow, like a drum, it is cooked. If it does not sound hollow, lower the oven temperature to fairly hot 375°F (Gas Mark 5, 190°C), return the loaf to the oven and bake for a further 5 to 10 minutes.

Cool the loaf on a wire rack.

French Bread

Although no butter, oil or sugar is used in the making of French bread, the other ingredients — flour, salt, yeast and water — are the same as those in other bread recipes. The unique taste, texture and appearance of French bread is achieved by slightly different methods and much longer proving times. To make French bread successfully you will need extra equipment: two smooth canvas pastry cloths or new linen cloths, a firm piece of cardboard, measuring 20-inches by 8-inches, and a very large baking sheet.

The ordinary French baguette is about 24-inches long and would be impossible to bake in a domestic oven, so the following recipe gives detailed instructions for making 3 bâtards, approximately 16-inches long and 3-inches wide. Because the dough is ovenproved and contains no butter or oil, French bread is best eaten on the day it is baked.

3 BATARDS

½ oz. fresh yeast
12½ oz. [1½ cups plus 1 tablespoon] lukewarm water
1 lb. [4 cups] strong flour
1¼ teaspoons salt

Crumble the yeast into a small bowl and add 2½ fluid ounces [¼ cup plus 1 tablespoon] of the lukewarm water. Cream the water and yeast together.

Put the flour and salt into a large mixing bowl. Make a well in the centre of the flour and pour in the yeast mixture and the remaining 10 fluid ounces [1¼ cups] of water. Using a spatula, gradually draw the flour into the liquid. Continue mixing the flour into the liquid until it forms a sticky dough.

Turn the dough out on to a lightly floured board or marble slab, making sure you scrape all the pieces of dough from the sides of the bowl. Leave the dough to rest for 3 minutes. Rinse and dry the mixing bowl and set it aside.

The dough will be stickier than other bread doughs at this stage. Knead it in the usual way for about 5 minutes, or until it is elastic and smooth, adding a sprinkling of flour if it remains too sticky. Let the dough rest for 3 minutes

and then knead it again for 2 minutes. The dough should still be very soft.

Shape the dough into a ball and return it to the mixing bowl. Cover the top of the bowl with a sheet of polythene [plastic] and place a thick towel over the polythene [plastic]. Set the bowl in a warm, draught-free place, with an approximate temperature of 70°F, and leave it for 3 hours, or until the dough has risen to about three and one-half times its original bulk. At this time the dough should have bubbles on the surface and will be spongy when touched.

Turn the risen dough out of the bowl on to a lightly floured surface, using a spatula to scrape the bowl clean. Lightly flour your hands and press the dough down and out into a circular shape, making sure all the bubbles are deflated.

Loosely fold the dough into a parcel and carefully place it back in the bowl. Cover it with the polythene [plastic] and the towel and return it to the same warm place for 2 to 3 hours, or until the dough has risen to almost three times its original bulk. It should again be spongy when touched.

Turn the risen dough out of the bowl on to the floured surface, and again press the dough down and out into a circular shape. Using a long, sharp knife, cut the dough into three pieces. Fold each piece of dough in half crosswise and set aside for 5 minutes.

Spread a well-floured canvas pastry cloth or linen cloth over a large tray or baking sheet.

Form the dough into three individual loaves. Leaving the other two loaves covered with a cloth, take the first piece of dough and press it firmly with your hands into an oval shape about 10-inches long. Neatly fold the dough in half lengthways and press the edges lightly together. Roll the dough over so that the seam is on top. Again press the dough into an oval shape the same size as the first oval and fold it in half as before. Seal the edges and roll the dough over so that the seam is underneath.

Place your hands in the centre of the roll, and gently rock it back and forth, working your hands out to the ends to form a sausage shape about 16-inches long, or to a length to fit your baking sheet. Place the rolled dough on to the floured cloth. Make a deep tuck in the cloth alongside the dough, forming a trough.

Shape and roll the remaining two pieces of dough in the same way, and lay them on the floured cloth, with a tuck between each.

Cover the dough with another floured cloth and place it in a very dry warm

place for about 1½ to 2 hours or until the dough has again risen to about three times its original bulk.

Preheat the oven to hot 425°F (Gas Mark 7, 220°C).

Transfer the loaves from the floured cloth on to the baking sheet, turning them upside-down so that the soft underside of the dough is face up on the baking sheet. This can be done easily by using a piece of floured cardboard to prise the dough from the cloth and then sliding the dough gently on to the baking sheet. Make sure that the loaves are straight and about 2½ to 3 inches apart.

Using a pastry brush, remove any excess flour from the surface of the loaves.

With a long sharp knife, make 3 long slashes in the top of each loaf.

Place the baking sheet a little above centre in the oven and bake for 30 minutes, or until the undersides of the loaves are a deep golden brown.

After removing the bread from the oven, slide the loaves off the baking sheet and rap the undersides with your knuckles. If the bread sounds hollow it is cooked.

Brioche

Made of yeast dough, a brioche (bree-yohsh) is a versatile bun that originated in France. Brioches may be baked in loaf or fluted tartlet tins, in the traditional round or ball shape with a round 'head', or they may be baked in a ring. Fresh brioches may be eaten with butter or jam. Stale brioches are delicious sliced and toasted.

Large brioches are often hollowed out and used as a container for sweet or savoury foods.

Brioche

The process used in making brioches is more complicated than that for most bread, and particular care must be taken in the early stages. Your efforts, however, will be rewarded, because brioches are the most delicious of buns. This traditional recipe may be used for either a Grosse Brioche à tête (grohs bree-yohsh ah tet) or the smaller individual Petites Brioches aux têtes (p'-teet bree-yohsh oh tet). Both have the classic 'heads'.

1 LARGE BRIOCHE OR 8 SMALL BRIOCHES

3 oz. [⅜ cup] butter
8 oz. [2 cups] flour
½ oz. yeast
1 teaspoon salt
2 teaspoons castor sugar
2 eggs

For Brioche, crumble the yeast into the flour, moistening with a little warm water to dissolve the yeast.

Gather the yeast dough into a compact ball and, with a sharp knife, cut a cross in the top.

Break the eggs into the remaining flour and gradually work in the milk to form a sticky dough.

Beat the dough for about 10 minutes, by drawing it up and throwing it down, until it is elastic.

Gradually work the butter into the dough, beating and mixing it vigorously, until it is smooth.

Mix the yeast ball into the dough and put the complete dough into a bowl. Cover the bowl and leave for 3 hours.

Place three-quarters of the dough in a brioche mould and, with your fingers, make a well in the centre.

Roll the remaining dough into a ball and firmly push it into the hole in the centre.

2 to 3 tablespoons milk
GLAZE
1 egg, lightly beaten

Place the butter on a marble slab or on a sheet of greaseproof or waxed paper on a board. Soften the butter by beating it with a rolling pin. Then spread it out with the heel of your hand until it is smooth and soft. Scrape the butter off the marble, or paper, with a knife and set it aside on a plate.

Clean the board or marble slab. Dry it thoroughly and then sift the flour on to it. Using your fingers, draw aside one-quarter of the flour and make a well in the centre. Crumble the yeast into the well and moisten it with only enough warm water to dissolve the yeast. Using your fingers, mix to a soft dough. Gather the dough into a ball and, with a knife, cut a cross in the top.

Slide the yeast ball into a bowl of lukewarm water. Be sure the water is not hot, or it will kill the yeast. Set the bowl aside for 8 minutes. In this time the yeast ball should rise to the surface and double in size. With your hand, scoop the yeast ball out of the bowl and drain it on a cloth. If your dough is not finished by the time the yeast ball is ready, cover it with an inverted mixing bowl until you are ready to use it.

Sprinkle the remaining flour with the salt and sugar. Make a well in the centre and into this break the eggs and add a little milk. Mix the eggs and milk together with your fingers and gradually draw in the flour. Continue mixing, adding more milk if necessary, until the mixture becomes a sticky dough.

Beat the dough with the fingers of one hand by drawing the dough up and then throwing it down again on to the board. Continue lifting, throwing, and scraping the dough back together again into a mass. After about 10 minutes of such beating, the dough should have enough elasticity and body so that it hardly sticks to your fingers.

Now begin to work the softened butter gradually into the dough. Add only about 2 tablespoons at a time. After each addition of butter, beat the dough, mix it vigorously with your fingers and smear it around on the board. When all the butter has been incorporated, the dough should be smooth and only barely sticky.

With your fingers, mix the drained yeast ball thoroughly into the dough. The consistency of the finished dough will be like that of stiffly whipped cream.

Scrape the dough off the board with a knife and gather it into a ball in your hands. Place it in a clean, lightly floured bowl that is large enough to allow the dough to double in size. Cover with a cloth and put the bowl in a warm place (80°F—85°F) for 3 hours.

At the end of this time, the dough will have doubled in bulk. Push the dough down with your fist, cover the bowl with aluminium foil and refrigerate for at least 4 hours, or overnight. An alternative method is to put the covered bowl directly into the refrigerator, instead of putting it in a warm place and leaving it to rise for at least 12 hours.

Remove the bowl from the refrigerator. The dough will now be firm enough to handle and is ready to be shaped, proved and baked.

To make a large brioche, butter a fluted 1-pint brioche mould or a baking sheet. Turn the dough out of the bowl on to a lightly floured board or marble slab. Knead the dough lightly with the heel of your hand. Form the dough into a roll.

With a knife, cut off one-quarter of the dough and roll the remaining three-quarters into a ball. Place this ball in the mould or on the baking sheet. Make a hole in the centre of the ball by inserting three fingers into it.

Roll the remaining quarter of dough into a ball and taper one side into a point. Firmly push this 'tail' into the hole in the larger ball.

With a knife, make a few shallow incisions in the large ball close under the 'head'. Cover the mould or baking sheet and put it in a warm place. Leave to rise again (to prove) for 15 minutes. The proving may also be done on a rack over a tin of boiling water.

Preheat the oven to very hot 475°F (Gas Mark 9, 240°C).

After proving, brush the surface of the brioche with beaten egg. Bake in the centre of the oven for 20 minutes until the brioche has risen and is beginning to brown. Reduce the oven temperature to moderate 350°F (Gas Mark 4, 180°C) and continue baking for 30 minutes. The brioche is done when the surface is golden brown and a knife plunged down into the centre comes out clean.

Take the brioche out of the oven and transfer it to a wire rack. Cool the brioche for 25 minutes before lifting it out of the mould.

To make small individual brioches, butter 8 small brioche moulds (fluted, deep, tartlet moulds). After the dough has been removed from the refrigerator, lightly kneaded and shaped into a roll, divide it into 8 egg-sized portions. Cut off one-third of each 'egg' with a knife and roll the remaining two-thirds of each 'egg' into balls. Place the balls in the moulds and make an indentation in the top of each ball with one finger.

Shape the remaining one-third of dough into smaller balls, tapering into tails, and push one into the indentation in each large ball. Place the filled moulds on a baking sheet and prove in a warm place for 15 minutes.

Preheat the oven to hot 425°F (Gas Mark 7, 220°C).

After proving, brush each brioche with beaten egg. Bake in the centre of the oven for 15 minutes. When done, the tops will be golden brown. Remove the baking sheet from the oven and transfer the moulds to a wire rack. Cool the brioches for 20 minutes before turning out.

Garlic Bread

☆ ① ✕

An excellent accompaniment to savoury dishes, Garlic Bread is very simple to make.

2 LOAVES

8 oz. [1 cup] butter, softened
2 tablespoons finely chopped fresh parsley
2 garlic cloves, very finely chopped
2 long loaves of French bread

Preheat the oven to fairly hot 400°F (Gas Mark 6, 200°C).

In a small mixing bowl, cream the butter, parsley and garlic together with a wooden spoon. With a large knife, thickly slice the loaves crosswise to within about ¼-inch of the bottom.

Spread the butter mixture generously on one side of each of the slices. Wrap the loaves in aluminium foil and place them on a baking sheet in the centre of the oven. Bake for 15 to 20 minutes, or until the bread is very crusty and the butter has melted.

Remove the loaves from the oven and serve immediately, in the foil.

Bread Sticks

☆ ① ✕ ✕ ✕

Bread sticks are nice to serve with soups or salads. They may be made with left-over ordinary bread dough, but the recipe given here, which is slightly richer than bread dough, will result in crunchier sticks. They will keep well if stored in an airtight tin. For an interesting variation, add ¼ teaspoon grated nutmeg, 1 teaspoon dried sage and 1 tablespoon caraway seeds to the dough before it is left to rise.

32 STICKS

8 fl. oz. [1 cup] milk
½ oz. yeast
1 teaspoon sugar
1 lb. [4 cups] flour
1 teaspoon salt
2 tablespoons butter
  milk or water (optional)
  crushed rock salt (optional)

Place the milk in a small saucepan and bring to just below the boiling point over moderately high heat. Remove the pan from the heat and allow the milk to cool to lukewarm.

Crumble the yeast into a small bowl. Add the sugar and cream it with the yeast. Stir in a little of the warmed milk to dissolve the yeast. Set the bowl in a warm place for 20 minutes. At the end of this time the yeast mixture will be frothy and almost doubled in bulk.

Sift the flour and salt into a warmed, medium-sized mixing bowl. Make a well in the centre of the flour and into this put the dissolved yeast.

Melt the butter in the warm milk and pour this into the well in the flour. Mix together the yeast mixture and the milk, and gradually draw in the flour. Continue mixing until a smooth dough is formed.

Cover the bowl with a clean cloth and leave the dough in a warm place to rise for 45 minutes.

When the rising is completed, turn the dough out on to a floured board or marble slab and knead it for 3 minutes until it is smooth.

Form the dough into a roll and cut it into 32 small pieces with a knife. Roll the pieces into sticks as thick as your little finger and 6 to 8 inches long. Place the sticks on a baking sheet and prove for 20 minutes.

Preheat the oven to fairly hot 400°F (Gas Mark 6, 200°C).

Bake the bread sticks in the oven for 10 minutes. Then lower the oven heat to moderate 350°F (Gas Mark 4, 180°C) and continue baking for a further 20 minutes. Remove the sheet from the oven and transfer the sticks to a wire rack to cool.

To make salted bread sticks, before they are completely cool, brush the sticks with a little milk or water and then sprinkle them with crushed rock salt.

One of the great traditional breads from America, New England Soda bread is delicious served warm with lots of butter.

28

Bran Bread

A nutritious bread that is ideal for slimmers, Bran Bread is both inexpensive and easy to make. Unlike other breads, it requires only one rising of only 30 minutes, so it can be made in the morning and will be ready at lunchtime.

ONE 2-POUND LOAF

1 teaspoon vegetable oil
1 oz. fresh yeast
½ teaspoon sugar
1 pint [2½ cups] lukewarm water
1½ lb. stone-ground wholemeal flour [6 cups wholewheat flour]
1 oz. [¼ cup] soya flour
1½ teaspoons salt
3 oz. [1 cup] plus 2 tablespoons bran

Lightly grease a baking sheet with the oil. Set aside.

Crumble the yeast into a small mixing bowl and mash in the sugar with a kitchen fork. Add 2 tablespoons of the water and cream the water and yeast together to form a smooth paste. Set the bowl aside in a warm, draught-free place for 15 to 20 minutes or until the yeast mixture has risen and is puffed up and frothy.

Put the flours and salt into a large mixing bowl. Add 3 ounces [1 cup] of the bran. Make a well in the centre and pour in the yeast mixture and remaining water. Using your hands or a spatula, gradually draw the flour mixture into the liquids. Continue mixing until all the flour is incorporated and the dough comes away from the sides of the bowl.

Turn the dough out on to a lightly floured board or marble slab and knead it for 10 minutes, reflouring the surface if the dough becomes sticky. The dough should then be elastic and smooth.

Shape the dough into a ball and place it on the baking sheet. Sprinkle the remaining bran on top. Cover the sheet with a clean, damp cloth and set it in a warm, draught-free place. Leave it for 30 minutes or until the dough has risen and expanded across the baking sheet.

Preheat the oven to hot 450°F (Gas Mark 8, 230°C).

Place the baking sheet in the oven and bake the bread for 1½ hours. Then lower the temperature to moderate 350°F (Gas Mark 4, 180°C) and continue baking for 10 minutes.

After removing the bread from the oven, tip the loaf off the baking sheet and rap the underside with your knuckles. If the bread sounds hollow, like a drum, it is cooked. If it does not sound hollow, return the loaf, upside-down, to the oven and bake for a further 5 to 10 minutes.

Cool the loaf on a wire rack.

Hickory Loaf

A marvellously tasty teabread, Hickory Loaf is equally delicious by itself or spread with butter. If you cannot obtain hickory nuts, walnuts or pecans may be substituted — although the taste will be slightly different.

ONE 8-INCH LOAF

2 oz. [¼ cup] plus 1 teaspoon butter softened
4 oz. [½ cup] sugar
3 eggs
5 fl. oz. [⅝ cup] sour cream
8 oz. [2 cups] flour
1 teaspoon baking powder
½ teaspoon salt
1 teaspoon ground allspice
½ teaspoon ground ginger
3 oz. [½ cup] hickory nuts, chopped
2 oz. [⅓ cup] sultanas or raisins

Preheat the oven to moderate 350°F (Gas Mark 4, 180°C). With the teaspoon of butter, lightly grease an 8-inch loaf tin and set aside.

In a large mixing bowl, cream the sugar and remaining butter together with a wooden spoon until the mixture is light and creamy. Add the eggs and sour cream, beating until the mixture is smooth.

Sift the flour, baking powder, salt, allspice and ginger into a medium-sized mixing bowl. Add it to the butter mixture, a little at a time, beating constantly until all the flour mixture has been added and the batter is thick and smooth. Stir in the nuts and sultanas or raisins.

Pour the batter into the prepared loaf tin and place the tin in the oven. Bake the loaf for 1 hour, or until a skewer inserted into the centre of the loaf comes out clean.

Remove the tin from the oven and allow the loaf to cool in the tin for a few minutes. Then run a knife around the edges of the tin and carefully turn the loaf out on to a wire rack to cool completely.

The cooled hickory loaf can either be served plain, or else spread thickly with butter. It is excellent for tea, or a quick snack.

New England Soda Bread

An old American recipe, New England Soda Bread is easy to make and simply delicious. Serve this brown bread still warm with lashings of butter and cheese, accompanied by a cool glass of beer.

2 LOAVES

2 teaspoons vegetable oil
4 oz. stale crustless bread, soaked

overnight in 12 fl. oz. [1½ cups] cold water
4 fl. oz. [½ cup] molasses
1 teaspoon salt
5 oz. [1 cup] corn meal
5 oz. [1¼ cups] rye flour
5 oz. [1¼ cups] coarse wholewheat flour
2 teaspoons bicarbonate of soda [baking soda]
4 fl. oz. [½ cup] cold water

Using a pastry brush, lightly oil two 1½-pint, round, plain moulds or pudding basins with the vegetable oil. Set aside.

Using the back of a wooden spoon, rub the soaked bread through a fine wire strainer into a medium-sized mixing bowl. Add the molasses to the puréed bread, mixing them well together with a wooden spoon. Set aside.

In another medium-sized mixing bowl, combine the salt, corn meal, rye flour, wholewheat flour and soda.

Make a well in the centre of the dry ingredients. Pour in the water and add the bread and molasses mixture. Using a wooden spoon, stir the mixture until all the ingredients are well combined.

Divide the mixture between the two moulds or basins. Cover them very securely with greased aluminium foil, tied tightly with string under the rim of each basin.

Place a rack in the bottom of a large, deep saucepan which is wide enough to hold both the basins. Put the basins on the rack and pour in enough boiling water to come halfway up around the basins. Cover the saucepan and place it over low heat. Steam the bread for 3 to 3½ hours, adding more water when necessary.

Preheat the oven to cool 300°F (Gas Mark 2, 150°C).

Lift the basins out of the saucepan. Remove the foil covers and place the basins in the oven. Bake the bread for 15 minutes. This will remove any excess moisture from the bread. Remove the basins from the oven and turn the bread out on to a wire rack. Serve warm or cold.

San Francisco Sourdough Bread

Sourdough Bread, like many other ethnic recipes, was probably taken to the New World by European immigrants, there, in time, to evolve into a genuine 'American' speciality. This version of Sourdough Bread comes from San Francisco and is famous throughout the United States. If you prefer, the loaves may be baked in the shape of French bread rather than in a round, as

suggested here — both are traditional. San Francisco Sourdough Bread has a moist, slightly chewy flavour and tastes quite magnificent with lots of butter and cheese.

TWO 1½-POUND LOAVES

3 lb. [12 cups] **strong white flour**
2 tablespoons sugar
1½ tablespoons salt
1½ pints [3¾ cups] water
2 tablespoons vegetable oil
1 teaspoon butter

SOURDOUGH STARTER

8 oz. [2 cups] strong white flour
4 oz. [½ cup] sugar
16 fl. oz. [2 cups] milk

First make the starter. In a large screw-top container, combine all the starter ingredients, beating with a fork until they form a smooth paste. Screw on the lid and set aside in a warm place for between 3 and 4 days.

Sift the flour, sugar and salt into a very large, warmed mixing bowl. Make a well in the centre and pour in the starter, water and oil. Using your fingers or a spatula, gradually draw the flour mixture into the liquids. Continue mixing until all the flour is incorporated and the dough comes away from the sides of the bowl.

Turn the dough out on to a lightly floured board or marble slab and knead it for 5 minutes, reflouring the surface if the dough becomes sticky. The dough should be elastic and smooth.

Rinse, thoroughly dry and lightly grease the large mixing bowl. Shape the dough into a ball and return it to the bowl. Cover it with a clean damp cloth and set it in a warm, draught-free place for 2 hours or until the dough has risen slightly.

Preheat the oven to fairly hot 375°F (Gas Mark 5, 190°C). With the teaspoon of butter, grease a large baking sheet and set aside.

Turn the dough out of the bowl on to a floured surface and knead it for about 10 minutes. Cut the dough into two equal pieces and shape each piece into a thick round, about 6-inches in diameter. With a sharp knife, make a deep cross on the top of each round.

Place the rounds, well spaced apart, on the prepared baking sheet and place the sheet in the oven. Bake the bread for 1 hour to 1 hour 10 minutes.

Remove the bread from the oven and tip the loaves off the baking sheet. Rap the undersides with your knuckles. If the bread sounds hollow, like a drum, it is cooked. If it does not sound hollow, lower the oven temperature to warm 325°F (Gas Mark 3, 170°C), return the loaves to the oven, upside-down, and bake for a further 5 to 10 minutes.

Cool the loaves on a wire rack.

Johnnycake

 ①

Johnnycake, one of the great traditional breads of the United States, is basically a simple-to-make corn meal bread.

ONE 8-INCH BREAD

2 oz. [¼ cup] butter, melted
4 oz. [1 cup] self-raising flour
1 teaspoon salt
1 teaspoon bicarbonate of soda [baking soda]
2 oz. [¼ cup] sugar
4 oz. [¾ cup] corn meal
2 eggs, lightly beaten
4 fl. oz. [½ cup] milk

Grease an 8-inch square baking tin with 1 tablespoon of the melted butter. Set aside.

Preheat the oven to fairly hot 400°F (Gas Mark 6, 200°C).

Sift the flour, salt and soda into a large mixing bowl. Add the sugar and the corn meal. Make a well in the centre and pour in the eggs, milk and the remaining melted butter. Using your fingers or a spatula gradually incorporate the dry ingredients and the liquids, mixing until they are well blended.

Spoon the batter into the baking tin, smoothing it down with a palette knife. Place the baking tin in the oven and bake for 20 to 25 minutes, or until the top is golden brown.

Remove the tin from the oven and allow the bread to cool before serving.

Boston Brown Bread

 ①

This is the authentic recipe for the unusual American steamed bread which was made in colonial New England. It is easy to prepare and, although it must steam for 3½ hours, it is well worth waiting for.

2 LOAVES

2 teaspoons vegetable oil
18 fl. oz. [2¼ cups] commercial buttermilk
6 fl. oz. [¾ cup] molasses, or dark treacle
6 oz. [⅞ cup] seedless raisins
6 oz. [1¼ cups] cornmeal
6 oz. [1¼ cups] rye flour
6 oz. [1¼ cups] wholewheat flour
2 teaspoons baking powder
1 teaspoon salt

Using a pastry brush, lightly oil two 2-

One of America's great traditional recipes, San Francisco Sourdough Bread is served with lots of butter.

pint, round, plain moulds or pudding basins.

Pour the buttermilk, molasses, or dark treacle, and raisins into a medium-sized mixing bowl and beat together.

Put the cornmeal, rye flour, whole-wheat flour, baking powder and salt into a large mixing bowl. Stir to mix. Pour in the buttermilk mixture and continue to stir until well mixed.

Divide the mixture between the two moulds or basins. Cover them very securely with greased aluminium foil, tied tightly with string under the lip of each basin.

Place a rack in the bottom of a large, deep saucepan which is wide enough to hold both the basins. Put the basins on the rack and pour in enough boiling water to come halfway up around the basins. Cover the saucepan and boil steadily, over moderate heat, for 3 to 3½ hours. Add more water when necessary to keep the water at the original level.

Preheat the oven to cool 300°F (Gas Mark 1-2, 150°C).

After taking the basins out of the saucepan, remove the foil covers and place the basins in the oven for about 15 minutes. This will remove any excess moisture from the bread.

Turn the bread out on to a rack. Serve hot or cold.

Moravian Loaf

This loaf, adapted from a traditional Czechoslovakian recipe, contains mashed potatoes. The bread is very light and may be served, slightly warm, with butter.

ONE 2-POUND LOAF

½ oz. fresh yeast
6 oz. [¾ cup] plus ½ teaspoon sugar
4 fl. oz. [½ cup] lukewarm water
1½ lb. [6 cups] flour
1 teaspoon salt
1 teaspoon ground cinnamon
5 oz. [⅝ cup] plus 1 teaspoon butter
8 oz. potatoes, cooked and mashed
3 tablespoons sugar mixed with 2 teaspoons grated nutmeg and ¼ teaspoon ground mace

Crumble the yeast into a small bowl and mash in the ½ teaspoon of sugar with a kitchen fork. Add 2 fluid ounces [¼ cup] of the water and cream the water and yeast together. Set the bowl aside in a warm, draught-free place for 15 to 20 minutes or until the yeast mixture is puffed up and frothy.

Sift the flour, salt, cinnamon and remaining sugar into a warmed, large mixing bowl. Add 3 ounces [⅜ cup] of

31

the butter. With a table knife, cut the butter into small pieces. Then, with your fingertips, rub the butter into the flour mixture until the mixture resembles coarse breadcrumbs.

Add the potatoes to the flour mixture. Make a well in the centre of the flour and potato mixture and pour in the yeast mixture and the remaining water. Using your fingers or a spatula, gradually draw the flour mixture into the liquids. Continue mixing until all the flour is incorporated and the dough comes away from the sides of the bowl.

Turn the dough out on to a lightly floured board or marble slab and knead it for 8 minutes, reflouring the surface if the dough becomes sticky. The dough should be smooth and elastic.

Rinse, thoroughly dry and lightly grease the large mixing bowl. Shape the dough into a ball and return it to the bowl. Cover the bowl with a clean damp cloth and set it in a warm, draught-free place. Leave it for 2 hours or until the dough has risen and almost doubled in bulk.

Lightly grease a 2-pound loaf tin with the 1 teaspoon of butter. Set aside.

Turn the risen dough out of the bowl. on to a floured surface and knead it for about 4 minutes. Shape the dough into an oblong shape and put it into the prepared tin.

In a small saucepan, melt the remaining butter over moderate heat. Remove the pan from the heat. With a pastry brush, brush the top of the dough with a little of the melted butter. Return the tin to a warm place for 30 minutes or until the dough has risen almost to the top of the tin. Brush the dough again with a little of the remaining melted butter during the rising time.

Preheat the oven to fairly hot 375°F (Gas Mark 5, 190°C).

Using a sharp knife, make three deep cuts in the top of the dough. Sprinkle the sugar and spice mixture into the cuts and pour in the remaining melted butter.

Place the tin in the centre of the oven and bake for 1 hour. If the loaf begins to look too brown, cover the top of the tin with aluminium foil.

Remove the tin from the oven, tip the loaf out of the tin and rap the underside with your knuckles. If the bread sounds hollow, like a drum, it is cooked. If it does not sound hollow, reduce the oven temperature to warm 325°F (Gas Mark 3, 170°C), return the loaf, upside-down, to the oven and bake for a further 4 minutes.

Remove the loaf from the oven and turn out on to a wire rack to cool. Serve slightly warm with butter.

Iranian Nut Bread

An excitingly different bread, Iranian Nut Bread has been made in the Middle East for centuries. It is perfect to serve with soups, salads or any Middle Eastern dish.

ONE 1-POUND LOAF

½ oz. fresh yeast
1 tablespoon plus ¼ teaspoon sugar
10 fl. oz. [1¼ cups] lukewarm milk
1 lb. [4 cups] flour
1 teaspoon salt
1 tablespoon oil
TOPPING
2 egg yolks, lightly beaten
2½ oz. [½ cup] chopped unblanched almonds, lightly toasted
2½ oz. [½ cup] chopped hazelnuts, lightly toasted
2½ oz. [½ cup] pine nuts, lightly toasted
2 tablespoons sesame seeds
½ tablespoon poppy seeds
¼ teaspoon ground cumin
½ teaspoon ground fennel
½ teaspoon black pepper
1 teaspoon coarse rock salt
2 oz. [½ cup] Parmesan or other hard cheese, finely grated

Crumble the yeast into a small mixing bowl and mash in ¼ teaspoon of the sugar with a fork. Add 1 tablespoon of the milk and cream the mixture together to form a smooth paste. Set the bowl aside in a warm, draught-free place for 15 to 20 minutes, or until the yeast mixture is puffed up and frothy.

Sift the flour, salt and remaining sugar into a medium-sized mixing bowl. Make a well in the centre and pour in the remaining luke warm milk, the oil and the yeast mixture.

Using your fingers or a spatula, mix the liquids together. Gradually draw the flour into the liquids and continue mixing until all the flour has been incorporated and the dough comes away from the sides of the bowl.

Turn the dough out on to a floured board or flat surface and knead it for 10 minutes, or until the dough is smooth and elastic.

Rinse, dry and lightly grease the mixing bowl. Shape the dough into a ball and sprinkle it with a little flour. Place the dough in the mixing bowl and cover it with a clean, damp cloth. Set it aside in a warm, draught-free place for 1 to 1½ hours, or until it has risen and almost doubled in bulk.

Turn the risen dough out on to a floured surface and knead it for about 5 minutes. Shape the dough into a ball.

Line a large baking sheet with non-

stick silicone paper. Place the ball of dough on the baking sheet and flatten it to form a flat circular shape.

Set the baking sheet aside while you make the topping.

In a medium-sized mixing bowl, combine the egg yolks, chopped nuts, sesame seeds, poppy seeds, cumin, fennel and pepper. With a wooden spoon mix all the ingredients well together.

Put the topping on to the centre of the dough and spread it out to within 1½-inches of the edge. Sprinkle the coarse salt over the topping and cover with the grated cheese.

Cover the dough with a clean, damp, cloth and set it aside in a warm place for 1 to 1½ hours or until it has risen and expanded across the baking sheet.

Preheat the oven to very hot 475°F (Gas Mark 9, 240°C).

Place the dough in the centre of the oven and bake for 15 minutes.

Reduce the oven temperature to hot 425°F (Gas Mark 7, 220°C). Place the baking sheet on the lowest shelf of the oven and bake for a further 30 to 35 minutes. After removing the bread from the oven, tip it off the baking sheet and rap the underside with your knuckles. If the bread sounds hollow, like a drum, it is cooked. If it does not sound hollow, return the loaf to the oven and bake for a further 5 to 10 minutes.

Transfer the bread to a wire rack to cool completely before serving.

Khachapuri

GEORGIAN CHEESE BREAD

A savoury cheese bread from Georgia, one of the southern republics of the U.S.S.R., Khachapuri (kha-chah-poor-ee) is so popular that individual breads are made and sold by hawkers in the streets. The individual breads are made in the form of open flans from circles of dough.

ONE 2 POUND LOAF

½ oz. fresh yeast
½ teaspoon sugar
4 to 5 fl. oz. [½ to ⅝ cup] lukewarm milk
1 lb. [4 cups] flour
1 teaspoon salt
3 oz. [⅜ cup] plus 1 teaspoon butter, melted
FILLING
1¾ lb. Caerphilly or any crumbly white cheese, crumbled

Khachapuri is a well-known Russian cheese bread. Serve it on its own or with salad meals, plain or buttered.

2 oz. [¼ cup] butter, softened
1 egg
1 egg yolk
1 teaspoon chopped fresh parsley

Crumble the yeast into a small bowl and mash in the sugar with a fork. Add 4 tablespoons of the milk and cream the milk and yeast together. Set the bowl aside in a warm, draught-free place for 15 to 20 minutes or until the yeast mixture is puffed up and frothy.

Sift the flour and salt into a warmed large mixing bowl. Make a well in the centre and pour in the yeast mixture, the remaining milk and 3 ounces [⅜ cup] of the butter. Using your fingers or a spatula, gradually draw the flour mixture into the liquids. Continue mixing until all the flour is incorporated and the dough comes away from the sides of the bowl without sticking.

Turn the dough out on to a lightly floured board or marble slab and knead it for 8 minutes, reflouring the surface if the dough becomes sticky. The dough should be elastic and smooth.

Rinse, thoroughly dry and lightly grease the large mixing bowl. Shape the dough into a ball and return it to the bowl. Cover the bowl with a clean damp cloth and set it in a warm, draught-free place. Leave it for 1 hour, or until the dough has risen and almost doubled in bulk.

Turn the risen dough out of the bowl on to a floured surface and knead it for about 3 minutes. Shape the dough into a ball and return it to the bowl. Cover and

leave for 1 hour, or until it has risen and almost doubled in bulk.

Meanwhile, prepare the filling. In a medium-sized mixing bowl, mash the cheese, butter, egg, egg yolk and parsley together, beating until the ingredients are well blended. Place the bowl in the refrigerator and chill the mixture until it is required.

With the remaining teaspoon of butter, lightly grease an 8-inch loose-bottomed cake tin and set it aside.

Turn the risen dough out of the bowl on to a floured surface and, with a rolling pin, roll it out into a circle, approximately 21 inches in diameter. Lift the dough circle carefully on the rolling pin and place it over the cake tin so that there is an even amount of dough hanging all around the tin. Gently ease the dough into the tin, leaving the excess dough hanging over the sides.

Remove the filling from the refrigerator and spoon it into the centre of the lined tin. With your fingers, draw the excess dough up and over the filling, pleating it into loose folds. Gather the dough in the centre and twist it into a small knob.

Preheat the oven to fairly hot 400°F (Gas Mark 6, 200°C).

Set the dough aside in a warm, draught-free place for 20 minutes, or until the dough has risen and increased in bulk.

Place the tin in the oven and bake the

bread for 30 minutes. Reduce the oven temperature to moderate 350°F (Gas Mark 4, 180°C) and bake for a further 20 minutes, or until the bread is well risen and deep golden in colour.

Remove the bread from the oven and leave it to cool in the tin for 30 minutes. Remove the sides and place the bread, still on the base of the tin, on a wire rack to cool completely.

Serve the bread cold.

Italian Mozzarella Bread

☆   ① ①   ◰

This savoury loaf not only tastes delicious — it looks superb. Serve it as an accompaniment to fondue or plain grilled [broiled] steaks.

ONE 1-POUND LOAF

1 teaspoon vegetable oil
1 x 1 lb. rye and caraway seed loaf
8 oz. mozzarella cheese
2 oz. [¼ cup] butter, softened
10 to 12 anchovies
12 black olives, halved and stoned
½ teaspoon dried marjoram
½ teaspoon dried basil

Preheat the oven to hot 425°F (Gas Mark 7, 220°C)' With the teaspoon of oil, lightly grease a large baking sheet. Set aside.

On a wooden board, slice the bread

Delicious with meat or soups, Italian Mozzarella Bread is made from rye and caraway bread, flavoured with olives, herbs, anchovies and cheese.

almost but not quite through to the base. The slices should be about ½-inch thick.

Cut the mozzarella into thin slices and insert the slices into the slices in the bread. With a flat bladed-knife, spread the top of the bread with the softened butter.

Place the anchovies over the top of the bread in a criss-cross pattern and decorate with the olives. Sprinkle over the marjoram and basil.

Place the loaf on the prepared baking sheet and place it in the oven. Bake for 15 minutes.

Remove the bread from the oven and serve immediately.

Spicy Cheese Bread

☆   ① ①   ◰ ◰ ◰

Spicy Cheese Bread is both nourishing and satisfying. Serve it with vegetable soup for an economical and filling meal, especially on cold days.

TWO 2-POUND LOAVES

¾ oz. fresh yeast
1 teaspoon sugar
2 tablespoons lukewarm water
12 fl. oz. [1½ cups] milk

1 oz. [2 tablespoons] butter or
    margarine
8 oz. wholemeal flour [2 cups
    wholewheat flour]
14 oz. [$3\frac{1}{2}$ cups] rye flour
1 teaspoon salt
1 teaspoon white pepper
$\frac{1}{8}$ teaspoon cayenne pepper
$\frac{1}{4}$ teaspoon dried thyme
1 egg
4 oz. [1 cup] Lancashire or other
    hard cheese, grated
2 teaspoons vegetable oil

Crumble the yeast into a small mixing bowl and mash in the sugar with a kitchen fork. Add the water and cream the yeast and water together to form a smooth paste. Set the bowl aside in a warm, draught-free place for 15 to 20 minutes or until the yeast mixture has risen and is puffed up and frothy.

Meanwhile, in a small saucepan, scald the milk over moderate heat (bring to just under boiling point). Remove the pan from the heat. Add the butter or margarine and set the pan aside to allow the milk to cool to lukewarm.

Put the flours, salt, pepper and cayenne into a warmed large mixing bowl and sprinkle over the thyme. Make a well in the centre of the flour mixture and pour in the yeast mixture, cooled milk mixture and the egg.

Using your fingers or a spatula, gradually draw the flour mixture into the liquids. Continue mixing until all the flour is incorporated and the dough comes away from the sides of the bowl. Add more flour if the dough is too sticky.

Add the cheese and lightly work it into the dough. Turn the dough out on to a lightly floured board or marble slab. Knead it for 10 minutes to distribute the cheese evenly. Reflour the surface if the dough is sticky. It should be elastic, stiff and smooth.

Rinse, thoroughly dry and lightly grease the large mixing bowl. Form the dough into a ball and return it to the bowl. Cover the bowl with a clean, damp cloth and set it aside in a warm, draught-free place for 1 to $1\frac{1}{2}$ hours, or until the dough has risen and almost doubled in bulk.

Lightly grease two 2-pound loaf tins with the oil. Set aside.

Turn the risen dough out of the bowl on to a floured surface and knead it for 8 to 10 minutes. Form the dough into a roll and with a sharp knife divide it into two equal pieces. Shape each piece into a loaf and place them in the tins. Cover the tins with a clean cloth and return them to a warm place for about 30 to 45 minutes, or until the dough has almost doubled in bulk again.

Preheat the oven to hot 425°F (Gas Mark 7, 220°C).

Place the tins in the centre of the oven and bake the loaves for 15 minutes. Then lower the temperature to fairly hot 375°F (Gas Mark 5, 190°C), put the tins on a lower shelf in the oven and continue baking for 30 to 35 minutes.

After removing the bread from the oven, tip the loaves out of the tins and rap the undersides with your knuckles. If the bread sounds hollow, like a drum, it is cooked, If it does not sound hollow, lower the oven temperature to moderate 350°F (Gas Mark 4, 180°C), return the loaves, upside-down, to the oven and bake for a further 5 to 10 minutes.

Cool the loaves on a wire rack. When the bread has cooled, it can be served with a vegetable soup as a nourishing economical meal in its own right. Otherwise serve with butter as usual, as a tasty snack.

Onion and Herb Loaf

Fragrant Onion and Herb Loaf is best made with fresh herbs. Dried herbs may be used in smaller quantities, but the aroma will not be as pungent, since drying does tend to change the flavour.

ONE 1-POUND LOAF

$\frac{1}{2}$ oz. fresh yeast
$\frac{1}{2}$ teaspoon sugar
4 fl. oz. [$\frac{1}{2}$ cup] lukewarm water
2 fl. oz. [$\frac{1}{4}$ cup] milk
1 tablespoon butter or margarine
10 oz. wholemeal flour [$2\frac{1}{2}$ cups
    wholewheat flour]
1 teaspoon salt
1 teaspoon finely chopped fresh sage
2 teaspoons finely chopped fresh
    tansy, wormwood or savory
1 small onion, minced
1 teaspoon vegetable oil

Crumble the yeast into a small mixing bowl and mash in the sugar with a kitchen fork. Add 2 tablespoons of the water and cream the yeast and water together to form a smooth paste. Set the bowl aside in a warm, draught-free place for 15 to 20 minutes or until the yeast mixture has risen and is puffed up and frothy.

Meanwhile, in a small saucepan scald the milk over moderate heat (bring to just under boiling point). Remove the pan from the heat and add the butter or margarine and the remaining water. Set the pan aside to allow the milk mixture to cool to lukewarm.

Put the flour and salt into a warmed large mixing bowl. Sprinkle over the herbs and onion. Make a well in the

centre of the flour mixture and pour in the yeast and milk mixtures. Using your fingers or a spatula, gradually draw the flour mixture into the liquids. Continue mixing until all the flour is incorporated and the dough comes away from the sides of the bowl.

Turn the dough out on to a lightly floured board or marble slab. Knead the dough for 10 minutes, reflouring the surface if the dough becomes sticky. The dough should then be elastic and smooth.

Rinse, thoroughly dry and lightly grease the large mixing bowl. Form the dough into a ball and return it to the bowl. Cover the bowl with a clean, damp cloth and set it aside in a warm, draught-free place for 1 to $1\frac{1}{2}$ hours or until the dough has risen and doubled in bulk.

Lightly grease a 1-pound loaf tin with the oil. Set aside.

Turn the dough out on to a floured surface and knead it for 8 to 10 minutes. Form the dough into a loaf and place it in the tin. Cover the tin with a cloth and return it to a warm place for 30 to 45 minutes or until the dough has doubled in bulk again.

Preheat the oven to moderate 350°F (Gas Mark 4, 180°C).

Place the tin in the centre of the oven and bake the bread for 1 hour.

After removing the bread from the oven, tip the loaf out of the tin and rap the underside with your knuckles. If the bread sounds hollow, like a drum, it is cooked. If it does not sound hollow, return the loaf, upside-down, to the oven and bake for a further 5 to 10 minutes.

Cool the loaf on a wire rack.

Herb Bread

Herb Bread is an unusual loaf which is easy and quick to make. Serve it hot with salads and fish dishes. A fresh white loaf or rolls can be substituted for French bread.

6 SERVINGS

1 large French loaf
6 oz. [$\frac{3}{4}$ cup] butter
1 garlic clove, crushed
1 tablespoon very finely chopped
    fresh parsley
$\frac{1}{4}$ teaspoon dried sage
1 tablespoon very finely chopped
    fresh chives
$\frac{1}{4}$ teaspoon black pepper

Preheat the oven to fairly hot 375°F (Gas Mark 5, 190°C).

Using a sharp knife, slice the bread downwards at 1-inch intervals to within $\frac{1}{4}$-inch of the base, so that each slice is still attached to the bottom of the crust.

Set aside.

In a small mixing bowl, cream the butter with a wooden spoon until it is smooth and creamy. Beat in the garlic, parsley, sage, chives and black pepper. Continue beating until the mixture is smooth and evenly coloured.

With a knife, spread equal amounts of the herb butter on to the bread slices, being careful not to detach them.

Wrap the loaf in aluminium foil and place it on a large baking sheet. Place the loaf in the centre of the oven and bake for 15 to 20 minutes, or until the loaf is very hot and the butter has melted into the bread.

Remove the loaf from the oven. Remove and discard the foil. Break the loaf into slices and serve immediately.

Herb Bread Crisps

These herb-flavoured bread snacks are ideal for serving in or with soups or with vegetable hors d'oeuvre.

4-6 SERVINGS

3 oz. [$\frac{3}{8}$ cup] butter
1 teaspoon lemon juice
$\frac{1}{2}$ teaspoon dried chervil
$\frac{1}{2}$ teaspoon dried tarragon
$\frac{1}{2}$ teaspoon chopped fresh parsley
$\frac{1}{4}$ teaspoon dried thyme
$\frac{1}{2}$ teaspoon chopped fresh chives
1 small garlic clove, crushed
6 slices of bread or 12 slices of
  French bread

Preheat the oven to moderate 350°F (Gas Mark 4, 180°C).

In a medium-sized mixing bowl, cream the butter with a wooden spoon until it is fairly soft. Stir the lemon juice into the butter and beat in the chervil, tarragon, parsley, thyme, chives and garlic.

Spread the butter mixture on the bread slices. If the slices are large, cut them in half diagonally. Place them on a baking sheet. Place the baking sheet in the oven and bake the bread for 20 minutes or until it is golden brown and crisp.

Remove the baking sheet from the oven and place the bread in a folded napkin in a basket. Serve immediately.

Rosemary Bread

An unusual accompaniment to cheese or soup, Rosemary Bread is delicious served

warm from the oven, spread with unsalted butter.

ONE 1-POUND LOAF

1 teaspoon butter
$\frac{1}{2}$ oz. fresh yeast
$\frac{1}{2}$ teaspoon sugar
10 fl. oz. [1$\frac{1}{4}$ cups] plus 1 tablespoon
  lukewarm water
12 oz. [3 cups] flour
1 teaspoon salt
4 oz. wholemeal flour [1 cup
  wholewheat flour]
1$\frac{1}{2}$ tablespoons plus 1 teaspoon
  dried rosemary

Grease a 1-pound loaf tin with the butter and set aside.

Crumble the yeast into a small bowl and mash in the sugar with a kitchen fork. Add the tablespoon of water and cream the water and yeast together. Set the bowl aside in a warm, draught-free place for 15 to 20 minutes or until the yeast mixture is puffed up and frothy.

Sift the flour and the salt into a warmed, large mixing bowl. Stir in the wholemeal [wholewheat] flour and the 1$\frac{1}{2}$ tablespoons of rosemary. Make a well in the centre and pour in the yeast mixture and the remain-

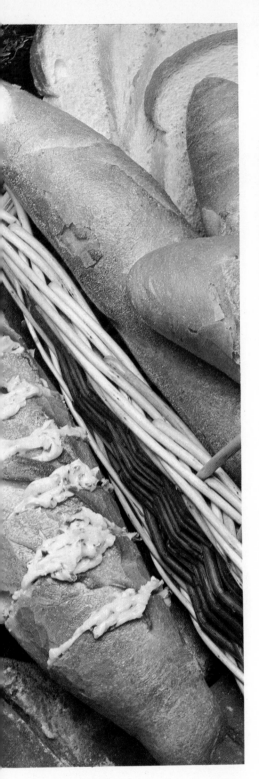

Rosemary Bread reflects the delicate flavour of this delicious herb.

it in a warm draught-free place for 1 to 1½ hours or until the dough has risen and has almost doubled in bulk.

Turn the dough out on to a floured surface and knead for about 3 minutes. Shape the dough into a loaf and place it in the tin. Return it to a warm, draught-free place for 30 to 45 minutes or until the dough has risen to the top of the tin.

Meanwhile, preheat the oven to very hot 475°F (Gas Mark 9, 240°C). Sprinkle the top of the dough with the remaining rosemary.

Place the tin in the centre of the oven and bake for 15 minutes. Then lower the temperature to fairly hot 375°F (Gas Mark 5, 190°C) and bake for a further 25 minutes.

After removing the bread from the oven, tip the loaf out of the tin and rap the underside with your knuckles. If the bread sounds hollow, like a drum, it is cooked. If it does not sound hollow, lower the oven temperature to warm 325°F (Gas Mark 3, 170°C), return the loaf, upside-down, to the oven and bake for a further 5 to 10 minutes.

Cool the loaf on a wire rack.

Poppy Seed Bread

☆ ☆　　① 　　✕ ✕ ✕

Poppy Seed Bread is a delicious white milky bread. *Traditionally the dough is braided before cooking, but it may be shaped into rounds or baked in a loaf tin.*

ONE 2-POUND LOAF

¾ oz. yeast
½ teaspoon sugar
16 fl. oz. [2 cups] lukewarm milk
2 lb. [8 cups] flour
2 teaspoons salt
4 oz. [½ cup] plus 1 teaspoon butter
1 egg, lightly beaten with 1 tablespoon milk
2 tablespoons poppy seeds

Crumble the yeast into a small bowl and mash in the sugar with a kitchen fork. Add 2 fluid ounces [¼ cup] of milk and cream the milk and yeast together. Set the bowl aside in a warm, draught-free place for 15 to 20 minutes or until the yeast mixture is puffed up and frothy.

Sift the flour and salt into a warmed, large mixing bowl. Add the 4 ounces [½ cup] of butter, and, using your fingertips, rub the fat into the flour until the mixture resembles fine breadcrumbs. Make a well in the centre and pour in the yeast mixture and remaining milk. Using your fingers or a spatula, gradually draw the flour mixture into the liquids. Continue mixing until all the flour is incorporated and the dough comes away from the sides of the bowl.

Turn the dough out on to a lightly floured board or marble slab and knead it for 10 minutes, reflouring the surface if the dough becomes sticky. The dough

ing water. Using your fingers or a spatula, gradually draw the flour mixture into the liquid. Continue mixing until all the flour is incorporated and the dough comes away from the sides of the bowl.

Turn the dough out on to a lightly floured board or marble slab and knead it for about 5 minutes, reflouring the surface if the dough becomes sticky. The dough should be elastic and smooth.

Rinse, thoroughly dry and lightly grease the large mixing bowl. Shape the dough into a ball and return it to the bowl. Cover the bowl with a clean damp cloth and set should be elastic and smooth.

Rinse, thoroughly dry and lightly grease the large mixing bowl. Shape the dough into a ball and return it to the bowl. Cover the bowl with a clean damp cloth and set it in a warm, draught-free place. Leave it for 1 to 1½ hours or until the dough has risen and has almost doubled in bulk.

Turn the risen dough out of the bowl on to a floured surface and knead it for about 8 minutes.

Using the remaining teaspoon of butter, grease a large baking sheet. Roll the dough out into a large oblong. Using a sharp knife, cut the dough, lengthways, into three equal strips, leaving the dough joined at one end. Braid the dough, then moisten the ends with water and press them together firmly. Carefully lift the dough braid on to the prepared baking sheet and return it to a warm place for 45 minutes to 1 hour or until the dough has almost doubled in bulk.

Preheat the oven to hot 425°F (Gas Mark 7, 220°C). Using a pastry brush, brush the dough with the egg and milk mixture and sprinkle with the poppy seeds.

Place the baking sheet in the centre of the oven and bake for 45 minutes.

Remove the baking sheet from the oven, tip the loaf off the baking sheet and rap the underside with your knuckles. If the bread sounds hollow, like a drum, it is cooked. If it does not sound hollow, reduce the oven temperature to warm 325°F (Gas Mark 3, 170°C), return the loaf to the oven and bake for a further 5 minutes.

Cool the loaf on a wire rack and serve.

Manitoba Poppy Seed Roll

A Canadian sweet bread filled with poppy seeds and honey, Manitoba Poppy Seed Roll is traditionally served at Christmas time.

1 ROLL

2 oz. [¼ cup] plus 1 teaspoon butter
¼ oz. fresh yeast
4 oz. [½ cup] plus ¼ teaspoon sugar
1 tablespoon lukewarm water
2 fl. oz. [¼ cup] lukewarm milk
8 oz. [2 cups] flour
1 teaspoon salt
3 egg yolks, lightly beaten
 grated rind of 1 lemon
POPPY SEED FILLING
2 oz. [¼ cup] unsalted butter
2 tablespoons clear honey
1 tablespoon double [heavy] cream
6 oz. [¾ cup] poppy seeds, roasted
2 oz. [⅓ cup] candied orange rind, finely chopped

4 oz. [⅔ cup] crushed almonds
1 egg white
GLAZE
1 egg yolk, lightly beaten

Grease a large baking sheet with the teaspoon of butter and set aside.

Crumble the yeast into a small bowl and mash in the ¼ teaspoon of sugar with a kitchen fork. Add the water and half the milk, and cream the liquids and yeast together to form a smooth paste. Set the bowl aside in a warm, draught-free place for 15 to 20 minutes, or until the yeast mixture is puffed up and frothy.

Pour the remaining milk into a medium-sized saucepan. Place it over low heat and add the remaining butter. When the butter has melted, remove the pan from the heat and allow the butter and milk mixture to cool to lukewarm.

Sift the flour, remaining sugar and the salt into a warmed large mixing bowl. Make a well in the centre of the flour mixture and pour in the yeast and milk and butter mixtures, the beaten egg yolks and lemon rind. Using your fingers or a spatula, gradually draw the flour into the liquid. Continue mixing until all the flour is incorporated and the dough comes away from the sides of the bowl.

Turn the dough out on to a floured board or marble slab and knead it for about 5 minutes, reflouring the surface if the dough becomes sticky. The dough should then be elastic and smooth.

Rinse, thoroughly dry and lightly grease the large mixing bowl. Shape the dough into a ball and return it to the bowl. Dust the top of the dough with a little flour and cover the bowl with a clean damp cloth. Set the bowl in a warm, draught-free place and leave it for 1 to 1½ hours or until the dough has risen and almost doubled in bulk.

Meanwhile prepare the poppy seed filling.

In a small mixing bowl, cream the butter and honey together with a wooden spoon. Add the cream. Stir in the poppy seeds, the orange rind and the almonds.

In a medium-sized mixing bowl, beat the egg white with a wire whisk or fork until it forms stiff peaks. Fold the egg white into the poppy seed mixture. Set aside.

Turn the risen dough out of the bowl on to a floured surface and knead it for about 4 minutes. Roll the dough out into a rectangle 14-inches by 8-inches and ½-inch thick.

Spoon the poppy seed mixture on to the dough and spread it out evenly, leaving a 1-inch border all round.

Carefully roll up the dough, Swiss [jelly] roll style. Gently press the end

down to prevent the roll from opening out. Place the roll on the baking sheet, seam side down. Cover with a cloth and return it to a warm place for 45 minutes, or until it has doubled in bulk.

Preheat the oven to moderate 350°F (Gas Mark 4, 180°C).

Brush the roll with the beaten egg yolk glaze.

Place the baking sheet in the centre of the oven and bake for 40 minutes or until the roll is deep golden brown.

Remove the baking sheet from the oven. Transfer the roll to a wire rack and set it aside to cool completely before serving.

Krendel
RUSSIAN NAME-DAY BREAD

Russians of the Orthodox faith are given

Manitoba Poppy Seed Roll is a traditional Canadian Christmas bread, filled with poppy seeds, nuts and honey.

Saints' names at their christenings, and thereafter they celebrate both their birthdays and their Name Days. Because there are a great many saints listed in the Russian calendar, a large family is likely to hold frequent parties, Krendel, a rich, very sweet fruit loaf, baked in the shape of a large B, is traditionally offered to friends and relatives when they drop in to offer Name Day congratulations. However, this attractive bread is delicious served for any occasion.

ONE 2-POUND LOAF

1 teaspoon plus 1 tablespoon
   butter, softened
½ oz. fresh yeast
8 oz. [1 cup] plus ¼ teaspoon sugar
1 tablespoon tepid water
4 fl. oz. [½ cup] milk
1 lb. [4 cups] flour
½ teaspoon salt
6 oz. [1 cup] sultanas or raisins
2 eggs, lightly beaten
8 oz. [1 cup] butter, chilled and cut
   into ⅛-inch slices

GLAZE

1 egg, lightly beaten
2 oz. [¼ cup] sugar

Grease a large baking sheet with the teaspoon of softened butter. Set aside.

Crumble the yeast into a small bowl and mash in the ¼ teaspoon of sugar with a fork. Add the water and cream the water and yeast together to form a smooth paste. Set the bowl aside in a warm, draught-free place for 15 to 20 minutes, or until the yeast mixture has risen and is puffed up and frothy.

Pour the milk into a small saucepan. Place it over moderately high heat and scald it (bring to just below boiling point). Reduce the heat to low and add the remaining tablespoon of butter. When the butter has melted, remove the pan from the heat and allow the milk and butter mixture to cool to lukewarm.

Sift the flour, remaining sugar and salt into a medium-sized mixing bowl. Stir in the sultanas or raisins. Make a well in the centre of the flour mixture and pour in the yeast mixture, the milk and butter mixture and the eggs. Using your fingers, or a spatula, gradually draw the flour into the liquid. Continue mixing until all the flour is incorporated and the dough comes away from the sides of the bowl.

Turn the dough out on to a floured board or marble slab and knead for about 10 minutes, reflouring the surface if the dough becomes sticky. The dough should then be elastic and smooth.

Rinse, thoroughly dry and lightly grease the mixing bowl. Shape the dough into a ball and return it to the bowl. Cover the bowl with a clean, damp cloth. Set the bowl in a warm, draught-free place and leave it for 1 to 1½ hours, or until the dough has risen and has almost doubled in bulk.

Turn the risen dough out of the bowl on to a floured surface and knead it for about 5 minutes. Flatten the dough out with the heel of your hand to an oblong about ¼-inch thick. Place the butter slices over about two-thirds of the dough and bring the other third of the dough over. Fold the dough over again so that the butter is completely enclosed. With a rolling pin, roll the dough out to an oblong ½-inch thick and fold in three again. Turn the dough so that the open end is facing you and roll out again. Repeat the folding and rolling twice more. With your hands, roll out the dough into a long sausage shape and twist it several times, like a rope.

Lay the twisted dough over the baking sheet so that equal lengths of dough hang over each end of the baking sheet. Bring the hanging pieces on to the baking sheet to form a large B-shape. Place a cloth over the baking sheet and return it to a warm place for about 30 to 45 minutes or until the dough has risen and expanded across the baking sheet.

Preheat the oven to moderate 350°F (Gas Mark 4, 180°C).

Using a pastry brush, brush the top of the dough with the beaten egg. Sprinkle the sugar evenly over the top. Place the baking sheet in the centre of the oven and bake for 35 to 40 minutes, or until the krendel is spread across the baking sheet and is golden brown.

Allow the krendel to cool on the baking sheet for 10 to 15 minutes before trans-

ferring it to a large wire rack.
Cool completely before serving.

Raisin Brown Bread

A really wholesome loaf to bake, Raisin Brown Bread is made with a mixture of stone-ground flour, treacle or molasses and rich Muscatel raisins. Serve warm from the oven, cut into slices and spread with butter.

TWO 1-POUND LOAVES

6 oz. [¾ cup] plus 2 teaspoons butter
¾ oz. fresh yeast
6 oz. [1 cup] plus 1 teaspoon soft
    brown sugar
3 teaspoons lukewarm water
16 fl. oz. [2 cups] milk
3 fl. oz. [⅜ cup] treacle or molasses
12 oz. [2 cups] Muscatel raisins,
    soaked in boiling water for 20
    minutes and drained
1 lb. stone-ground wholemeal
    flour [4 cups stone-ground
    wholewheat flour]
1 lb. [4 cups] stone-ground rye flour
1½ teaspoons salt

Grease two 1-pound loaf tins with the 2 teaspoons of butter and set aside.

Crumble the yeast into a small bowl and mash in the 1 teaspoon of sugar with a kitchen fork. Add the water and cream the water and yeast together to form a smooth paste. Set the bowl aside in a warm, draught-free place for 15 to 20 minutes or until the yeast has risen and is puffed up and frothy.

Meanwhile, pour the milk into a medium-sized saucepan and add the treacle or molasses. Scald the mixture over moderately high heat (bring to just below boiling point). Stir in the remaining butter and the remaining sugar, and stir until the butter has melted and the sugar dissolved. Remove the pan from the heat and set aside to cool to lukewarm.

Place the raisins in a warmed, large mixing bowl. Add the wholemeal [wholewheat] flour, rye flour and salt to the raisins and stir well to mix.

Make a well in the centre of the flour mixture and pour in the yeast and milk mixtures. Using your fingers or a spatula, gradually draw the flour into the liquid. Continue mixing until all the flour is incorporated and the dough comes away from the sides of the bowl.

Turn the dough out on to a floured board or marble slab and knead for about 10 minutes, reflouring the surface if the dough becomes sticky. The dough should be elastic and smooth.

Rinse, thoroughly dry and lightly grease the large mixing bowl. Shape the dough into a ball and return it to the bowl. Dust the top of the dough with a little flour and cover the bowl with a clean damp cloth. Put the bowl in a warm, draught-free place for 1½ to 2 hours or until the dough has risen and has almost doubled in bulk.

Turn the risen dough out of the bowl on to a floured surface and knead vigorously for about 4 minutes. Using a sharp knife, cut the dough in half. Roll and shape each piece of dough into a loaf and place in the tins. Cover with a damp cloth and return to a warm place for about 30 to 45 minutes or until the dough has risen slightly.

Preheat the oven to very hot 475°F (Gas Mark 9, 240°C).

Place the tins in the centre of the oven and bake for 15 minutes. Then lower the oven temperature to hot 425°F (Gas Mark 7, 220°C). Put the tins on a lower shelf in the oven and bake for another 25 to 30 minutes.

After removing the bread from the oven, tip the loaves out and rap the undersides with your knuckles. If the bread sounds hollow, like a drum, it is cooked. If the bread does not sound hollow, lower the oven temperature to fairly hot 375°F (Gas Mark 5, 190°C), return the loaves, upside-down, to the oven, and bake for a further 10 minutes.

Cool the loaves on a wire rack.

Easter Bread

Easter is an important festival in the Greek Orthodox Church, and they, like the Russians, end the Lenten fast with a long and enthusiastic celebration. This Greek bread is served as part of the Easter Saturday feast. The loaf is sometimes decorated with bright red eggs — hard-boiled in red food colouring. The rich warm flavour of the bread is enhanced by fresh lemon and crunchy sesame seeds.

ONE 2-POUND LOAF

5 oz. [⅝ cup] plus 1 teaspoon butter
¾ oz. fresh yeast
6 oz. [¾ cup] plus ½ teaspoon sugar
10 fl. oz. [1¼ cups] plus 2 teaspoons
    milk, lukewarm
2 lb. [8 cups] flour
1 teaspoon salt
6 egg yolks, lightly beaten
4 oz. [⅔ cup] chopped candied peel
    finely grated rind of 1 lemon
    finely grated rind of ½ orange
3 oz. [⅜ cup] sesame seeds

GLAZE

1 egg yolk beaten with 1
tablespoon cold water

Grease a large baking sheet with the teaspoon of butter. Set aside.

Crumble the yeast into a small bowl and mash in the ½ teaspoon of sugar with a fork. Add the 2 teaspoons of lukewarm milk and cream the milk and yeast together. Set the bowl aside in a warm, draught-free place for 15 to 20 minutes, or until the yeast mixture has risen and is puffed up and frothy.

Pour the remaining milk into a small saucepan and place it over moderately high heat. Bring it to just below boiling point. Reduce the heat to low and add the remaining butter, cut into small pieces. Stir the mixture with a wooden spoon until all the butter has melted. Remove the pan from the heat and allow the milk and butter mixture to cool to lukewarm.

Sift the flour, the remaining sugar and the salt into a large, warmed mixing bowl. Make a well in the centre of the flour mixture and pour in the yeast mixture, the milk and butter mixture and the egg yolks. Using your fingers or a spatula, gradually draw the flour into the liquid. Continue mixing until all the flour is incorporated and the dough comes away from the sides of the bowl. Mix in the candied peel and the grated lemon and orange rind.

Turn the dough out on to a lightly floured board or marble slab and knead it gently for about 5 minutes, reflouring the surface if the dough becomes sticky. The dough should then be elastic and smooth.

Rinse, thoroughly dry and lightly grease the large mixing bowl. Shape the dough into a ball and return it to the bowl.

Cover the bowl with a clean cloth. Set the bowl in a warm, draught-free place and leave it for 1 to 1½ hours, or until the dough has risen and has almost doubled in bulk.

Turn the risen dough out of the bowl on to a floured surface and knead it for about 5 to 8 minutes. Divide the dough into 3 pieces. Roll each piece, with your hands, into a sausage shape about 12-inches long, slightly tapering at the ends.

Sprinkle one-third of the sesame seeds on to the surface and roll one piece of the dough in the seeds, making sure the dough is well coated on all sides. Repeat this with the remaining sesame seeds and 2 pieces of dough.

Join the 3 pieces of dough into a loose plait [braid] and tuck the ends underneath. Put the plait [braid] on the baking sheet, cover with a clean cloth and set aside in a warm, draught-free place for 2

to 3 hours, or until the dough has almost doubled in bulk.

Preheat the oven to fairly hot 400°F (Gas Mark 6, 200°C).

With a pastry brush, paint the top of the loaf with the glaze. Place the baking sheet in the centre of the oven and bake for 10 minutes. Then lower the temperature to moderate 350°F (Gas Mark 4, 180°C) and continue baking for another 30 minutes, or until the bread is golden brown.

After removing the bread from the oven, leave it to cool on the baking sheet for 30 minutes, then transfer it to a wire rack to cool completely.

Easter Festival Bread

☆ ✡ ① ① ① ⋈ ⋈ ⋈

In Russia, this fruit bread is called kulich (koo-leech) *and is one of the traditional foods cooked for the Russian Orthodox Easter celebrations. However, there is no need to wait until Easter to make this richly flavoured bread; it would be ideal for any occasion. The bread should be cut horizontally into thin slices and the top replaced to prevent the bread from becoming dry.*

ONE 3-POUND LOAF

1½ oz. fresh yeast
¼ teaspoon sugar
7 fl. oz. [⅞ cup] milk, lukewarm
2 oz. [⅓ cup] raisins
3 tablespoons rum
1½ lb. [6 cups] flour
9 oz. icing sugar [2¼ cups confectioners' sugar]
½ teaspoon salt
½ teaspoon vanilla essence
9 egg yolks
8 oz. [1 cup] unsalted butter, softened
½ teaspoon saffron, soaked in 1 tablespoon hot water
1 teaspoon vegetable oil
2 oz. [½ cup] blanched, slivered almonds
2 oz. [⅓ cup] chopped candied peel
1½ oz. [3 tablespoons] butter
ICING
8 oz. icing sugar [2 cups confectioners' sugar]
3 tablespoons cold water
1 teaspoon lemon juice

Crumble the yeast into a small bowl and mash in the ¼ teaspoon of sugar with a fork. Add 1 tablespoon of the lukewarm milk and cream the milk and yeast together to form a smooth paste. Set the bowl aside in a warm, draught-free place for 15 to 20 minutes or until the yeast mixture has risen and is puffed up and frothy.

Topped with icing, this Russian Easter Festival Bread is rich with rum, almonds, eggs and fruit.

Place the raisins in a small bowl and cover them with the rum. Leave the raisins to soak for 15 minutes.

Sift the flour, the icing [confectioners'] sugar and the salt into a large, warmed mixing bowl. Make a well in the centre and pour in the remaining milk and the yeast mixture. Using your fingers or a wooden spoon, gradually draw the flour into the liquid. Continue mixing until all the flour has been incorporated. Then beat in the vanilla essence and the egg yolks, one at a time. Gradually beat the softened butter into the mixture.

Stir in the dissolved saffron and continue mixing until the ingredients are well blended and a smooth dough is formed.

Turn the dough out of the bowl on to a lightly floured board or marble slab and knead it for 10 minutes. Pull and stretch the dough well to make it smooth and elastic.

If, after 8 to 10 minutes of kneading, the dough is still sticky, add a little extra flour to make a smooth, soft, non-sticky dough.

Rinse, thoroughly dry and lightly grease the large bowl with the oil. Form the dough into a ball and place it in the bowl. Cover the bowl with a cloth and leave in a warm, draught-free place for 1½ hours or until the dough has doubled in bulk.

Preheat the grill [broiler] to moderate.

Put the almonds on the grill [broiler] pan and lightly toast them under the grill [broiler] until they are golden brown all over. Transfer the almonds to the bowl containing the soaked raisins and add the candied peel.

With 1 tablespoon of the butter, lightly grease a 2 pound coffee tin or a tall cylindrical mould, about 6 inches across and 7-inches high. Line it with grease-proof or waxed paper greased with the remaining butter. Allow the excess paper to come up over the rim of the tin. Place the tin or mould on a baking sheet.

Add the soaked fruit and nut mixture to the dough and fold the dough over the fruit and nuts. Knead the dough gently to distribute the fruit and nuts evenly.

Preheat the oven to fairly hot 400°F (Gas Mark 6, 200°C).

Form the dough into a ball again and place it in the tin or mould. Cover the tin or mould with a cloth and put it in a warm, draught-free place to rise for 30 minutes or until it has doubled in bulk.

Place the tin or mould, on the baking

sheet, in the oven. Bake for 40 minutes. Then lower the oven temperature to moderate 350°F (Gas Mark 4, 180°C) and continue baking for 1 hour.

Remove the bread from the oven and allow it to cool in the tin for 10 minutes. Then remove it from the tin and allow it to become completely cold, standing upright, on a wire rack.

To make the icing, sift the icing [confectioners'] sugar into a medium-sized bowl. Add the water and lemon juice and mix to a thin paste.

Pour the icing on to the top of the cooled bread and allow it to trickle down the sides. Allow the icing to set before serving.

Christmas Bread

A large, dark loaf with an unusual flavour Christmas Bread is an old traditional Swedish recipe. The bread is served at lunch on the day before Christmas, and is usually decorated with softened unsalted butter piped on top in a decorative pattern. Christmas Bread is particularly delicious with butter and cheese or honey. Try it for a change.

THREE 1-POUND LOAVES

¾ oz. fresh yeast
½ teaspoon brown sugar
2 tablespoons lukewarm water
1 pint [2½ cups] stout or dark brown ale
2 oz. [¼ cup] plus 1 tablespoon butter or margarine
1½ lb. [6 cups] rye flour
12 oz. [3 cups] flour
1 teaspoon salt
8 fl. oz. [1 cup] molasses
grated rind of 4 oranges
2 tablespoons aniseed, crushed
GLAZE
1 tablespoon molasses mixed with 3 tablespoons hot water

Crumble the yeast into a small mixing bowl and mash in the sugar with a kitchen fork. Add the water and cream the yeast and water together. Set the bowl aside in a warm, draught-free place for 15 to 20 minutes, or until the yeast mixture has risen and is puffed up and frothy.

Meanwhile, in a medium-sized saucepan, warm the stout or ale over low heat. Add 2 ounces [¼ cup] of the butter or margarine and heat the mixture for 2 to 3 minutes or until it is just lukewarm and the butter or margarine has melted. Remove the pan from the heat.

Sift the flours and salt into a large mixing bowl. Make a well in the centre and pour in the yeast and stout mixtures, the molasses, the orange rind and the aniseed. Using your fingers or a spatula, gradually draw the flour into the liquid. Continue mixing until all the flour is incorporated and the dough comes away from the sides of the bowl.

Turn the dough out on to a lightly floured board and knead it for 5 minutes, reflouring the surface if the dough is sticky. It should be elastic and smooth.

Rinse, thoroughly dry and lightly grease the large mixing bowl. Form the dough into a ball and return it to the bowl. Cover the bowl with a clean cloth and set it aside in a warm, draught-free place for 1½ to 2 hours, or until the dough has risen and almost doubled in bulk.

Lightly grease three baking sheets with the remaining tablespoon of butter or margarine. Set aside.

Turn the risen dough out on to a lightly floured surface and knead it for 10 minutes. Divide the dough into three equal pieces and shape each piece into a long loaf, slightly shorter than the baking sheets. Transfer the loaves to the baking sheets and cover them with clean cloths. Return them to a warm place for 45 minutes to 1 hour, or until the loaves have risen and expanded across the sheets.

Preheat the oven to very cool 250°F (Gas Mark ½, 130°C).

Uncover the loaves and prick them all over with a fork. Place the baking sheets in the oven and bake for 20 minutes.

Remove the loaves from the oven and brush them with the molasses and water glaze. Return the loaves to the oven and bake for a further 20 minutes.

After removing the bread from the oven, tip the loaves off the baking sheets and rap the undersides with your knuckles. If the bread sounds hollow, like a drum, it is cooked. If it does not sound hollow, return the loaves to the oven and bake for a further 10 to 15 minutes.

Cool the loaves on a wire rack.

Birnbrot

PEAR BREAD

The Swiss are famous for their cakes and pastries. Birnbrot (beern-broht), a pear tea bread, is usually accompanied by steaming cups of hot chocolate. If dried pears are not available, you can use canned or fresh pears, well drained and diced.

ONE LARGE LOAF

BREAD
2 oz. [¼ cup] plus 1 teaspoon sugar
5 fl. oz. [⅝ cup] lukewarm milk
1 tablespoon dried yeast
10 oz. [2½ cups] flour
⅛ teaspoon salt
2 oz. [¼ cup] plus 1 tablespoon butter
1 egg, lightly beaten
beaten egg and milk for glaze
FILLING
8 fl. oz. [1 cup] water
8 oz. [1⅓ cups] dried pears, coarsely chopped
4 oz. [⅔ cup] stoned, dried prunes, coarsely chopped
2½ oz. [½ cup] seedless raisins
juice of ½ lemon
2 oz. [½ cup] walnuts, chopped
2 tablespoons sugar
2 tablespoons kirsch
grated rind of 1 lemon
¼ teaspoon ground cinnamon
¼ teaspoon ground nutmeg
1½ tablespoons dry red wine

In a small bowl, dissolve 1 teaspoon of sugar in the lukewarm milk. Sprinkle the yeast on the milk and stir to mix. Let the mixture stand in a warm, draught-free place for about 10 minutes, or until the yeast bubbles up and the mixture almost doubles in bulk.

Sift the flour, salt and the remaining sugar into a large, warm mixing bowl. Rub 2 ounces [¼ cup] butter into the flour mixture with your fingertips. Make a well in the middle of the flour mixture and pour in the yeast and the lightly beaten egg. Stir to mix with a wooden spoon. Then, using your hands, lightly knead and pat the dough into a ball.

Turn the dough out on to a lightly floured surface and knead for 10 minutes, sprinkling the surface with a little extra flour when necessary to prevent the dough from sticking.

Shape the dough into a ball and place it in a large, greased bowl. Cover the bowl with a cloth and place it in a warm, draught-free place for 45 minutes or until the dough doubles in bulk.

While the dough is rising, prepare the filling. In a small saucepan bring the water to the boil. Add the pears, prunes, raisins and lemon juice to the water and, stirring frequently, simmer over low heat for 10 minutes, or until the fruit is tender and can be mashed easily with the back of a spoon.

Drain the fruit thoroughly. Purée it in a blender or rub it through a strainer with the back of a spoon. Stir the walnuts, sugar, kirsch, grated lemon rind, cinnamon and nutmeg into the fruit purée.

When the ingredients are well mixed, stir in the wine a little at a time. The purée should be very thick, so add the wine with caution.

Using a pastry brush, evenly coat a large baking sheet or Swiss-roll tin with

the remaining tablespoon of butter.

Lightly dust a piece of greaseproof or waxed paper, which is about 18-inches square, with flour. Punch the dough to get rid of air pockets. Transfer it to the paper. Knead the dough lightly and roll it into a square about $\frac{1}{4}$-inch thick.

With a palette knife, spread the filling over the dough, covering it smoothly to within 1 inch of its edges. Fold the edges over the filling and roll the dough like a Swiss [jelly] roll using the paper to lift the dough.

Rumanian Sweet Bread

Rumanian Sweet Bread is simply delicious sliced and spread with soft creamy butter and strawberry jam.

TWO 1-POUND LOAVES

6 oz. [$\frac{3}{4}$ cup] plus 2 teaspoons
 butter, cut into small pieces
$\frac{3}{4}$ oz. fresh yeast
6 oz. [$\frac{3}{4}$ cup] plus 1 teaspoon sugar
3 tablespoons lukewarm water
4 fl. oz. [$\frac{1}{2}$ cup] milk
2 lb. [8 cups] flour
1 teaspoon salt
4 fl. oz. [$\frac{1}{2}$ cup] sour cream
4 eggs, well beaten
TOPPING
2 egg yolks, well beaten
1 tablespoon brandy
2 oz. [$\frac{1}{3}$ cup] soft brown sugar
1 teaspoon ground allspice
2 oz. [$\frac{1}{3}$ cup] blanched almonds,
 chopped

Grease two 1-pound loaf tins with the 2 teaspoons of butter. Set aside.

Crumble the yeast into a small mixing bowl and mash in the 1 teaspoon of sugar with a kitchen fork. Add the water and cream the water and yeast together to form a smooth paste. Set the bowl aside in a warm, draught-free place for 15 to 20 minutes or until the yeast is puffed up and frothy.

Meanwhile, scald the milk over moderate heat (bring to just below boiling point). Add the remaining butter and remove the pan from the heat. Set aside until the butter has melted and the mixture has cooled to lukewarm.

Sift the flour and salt into a warmed, large mixing bowl and stir in the remain-

A soft, sweet white bread made with sour cream and eggs, Rumanian Sweet Bread tastes delicious with butter and home-made strawberry jam.

ing sugar. Make a well in the centre of the flour mixture and pour in the yeast, the milk and butter mixture, sour cream and eggs. Using your fingers or a spatula, mix the liquids together, gradually drawing in the flour. Continue mixing until all the flour is incorporated and the dough comes away from the sides of the bowl.

Turn the dough out on to a floured board or marble slab and knead for 10 minutes, reflouring the surface if the dough becomes sticky. The dough should be elastic and smooth.

Rinse, thoroughly dry and lightly grease the large mixing bowl. Shape the dough into a ball and return it to the bowl. Dust the top of the dough with a little flour and cover the bowl with a clean damp cloth. Set the bowl in a warm, draught-free place for 1 to $1\frac{1}{2}$ hours or until the dough has risen and has almost doubled in bulk.

Turn the risen dough out of the bowl

on to a floured surface and knead it for 4 minutes. Using a sharp knife, cut the dough into 2 pieces. Shape each piece into a loaf. Place the loaves in the tins, cover with a damp cloth and return to a warm, draught-free place for 30 to 45 minutes or until the dough has risen to the tops of the tins.

Meanwhile, make the topping. Place the egg yolks, brandy, sugar and allspice in a small mixing bowl and beat well with a wooden spoon. Set aside.

Preheat the oven to very hot 475°F (Gas Mark 9, 240°C). Place the loaves in the oven and bake for 15 minutes. Lower the temperature to hot 425°F (Gas Mark 7, 220°C).

Remove the loaves from the oven. Using a pastry brush, coat the tops generously with the egg yolk mixture and sprinkle over the almonds.

Return the loaves to the oven and bake for a further 20 to 30 minutes or until the loaves are cooked and the undersides sound hollow when rapped with your knuckles.

Remove the loaves from the oven and set them aside to cool in the tins for 10 minutes before turning them out on to a wire rack to cool completely.

Banana Walnut Loaf

A moist bread, Banana Walnut Loaf is very easy to make and good to serve at tea-time or with coffee.

ONE 9-INCH LOAF

5 oz. [⅝ cup] sugar
3 tablespoons plus 1 teaspoon vegetable fat
3 eggs
4 bananas, mashed
8 oz. [2 cups] sifted flour
1 teaspoon baking powder
½ teaspoon salt
¼ teaspoon bicarbonate of soda [baking soda]
6 oz. [1 cup] walnuts, chopped

Preheat the oven to moderate 350°F (Gas Mark 4, 180°C). Grease a 9-inch loaf tin with 1 teaspoon fat.

In a medium-sized mixing bowl, beat the sugar, vegetable fat and eggs together with a wooden spoon. Beat until it is

---

More a cake than a bread, this Banana Walnut Bread is quick, easy and inexpensive to make.

light. Beat in the bananas.

Sift the flour, baking powder, salt and soda into the banana mixture and beat well. Stir in the walnuts.

Pour the mixture into the loaf tin and bake for 1 hour, or until the loaf is done. Test by inserting a warm, dry skewer in the centre of the loaf. If it comes out clean, the loaf is ready. Turn the loaf out of the tin and allow to cool before slicing.

Poteca

SWISS YEAST CAKE

A delicious sweet bread filled with a chewy walnut cream, Poteca (poh-tay-kah) may be served sliced and spread with butter.

TWO 1-POUND LOAVES

¾ oz. fresh yeast
4 oz. [½ cup] plus ½ teaspoon sugar
3 teaspoons lukewarm water
8 fl. oz. [1 cup] milk
4 oz. [½ cup] plus 2 teaspoons butter
1½ lb. [6 cups] flour
1 teaspoon salt
2 egg yolks, lightly beaten
FILLING
3 egg whites

4 oz. [½ cup] castor sugar
6 oz. [1 cup] walnuts, very finely
   chopped
   grated rind of 1 small orange
   grated rind of 1 lemon
TOPPING
2 to 3 tablespoons clear honey,
   warmed
12 walnut halves
6 glacé cherries, halved
2 angelica strips, cut into small
   pieces

Crumble the yeast into a small bowl and mash in the ½ teaspoon of sugar with a kitchen fork. Add the water and cream the water and yeast together. Set the bowl aside in a warm, draught-free place for 15 to 20 minutes or until the yeast mixture is puffed up and frothy.

Pour the milk into a small saucepan. Place it over moderately high heat and scald the milk (bring to just under boiling point). Reduce the heat to low and add the 4 ounces [½ cup] of butter. When the butter has melted, remove the pan from the heat and allow the milk and butter mixture to cool to lukewarm.

Sift the flour, remaining sugar and salt into a warmed, large mixing bowl. Make a well in the centre of the flour mixture and pour in the yeast mixture, milk and butter mixture and the egg yolks.

Using your fingers or a spatula,

gradually draw the flour into the liquid. Continue mixing until all the flour is incorporated and the dough comes away from the sides of the bowl.

Turn the dough out on to a lightly floured board or marble slab and knead it for 10 minutes, reflouring the surface if the dough becomes sticky. The dough should be elastic and smooth.

Rinse, thoroughly dry and lightly grease the large mixing bowl. Shape the dough into a ball and return it to the bowl. Cover the bowl with a clean damp cloth and set it in a warm, draught-free place. Leave it for 1 to 1½ hours or until the dough has risen and doubled.

Meanwhile, using the 2 teaspoons of butter, grease two baking sheets.

In a medium-sized mixing bowl, beat the egg whites with a wire whisk or rotary beater until they form soft peaks. Using a metal spoon, carefully fold in the sugar, a little at a time. Beat the mixture until it is stiff and glossy. Fold in the walnuts and the orange and lemon rinds. Set aside.

Turn the risen dough out of the bowl on to a floured surface and knead it for about 5 minutes. Using a sharp knife, cut the dough into 2 pieces. Roll each piece of dough out to form a large, long rectangle. With a palette knife or spatula, spread half the filling on each piece of dough. With one of the long ends towards you, roll up each piece of dough Swiss [jelly]

Poteca is a very attractive sweet bread from Switzerland. Serve it sliced, on its own or with butter.

roll style. Carefully transfer the rolls to the prepared baking sheets, seam side down. Pull the ends of each loaf round to meet each other and make a circle. Wet the ends with a little water and press them together to seal, overlapping slightly.

Return the baking sheets to a warm place for about 30 to 45 minutes or until the dough has almost doubled in bulk.

Preheat the oven to hot 425°F (Gas Mark 7, 220°C).

Place the baking sheets in the oven and bake for 15 minutes.

Reduce the heat to moderate 350°F (Gas Mark 4, 180°C) and continue baking for a further 40 minutes. After removing the bread from the oven, tip the loaves off and rap the undersides with your knuckles. If the bread sounds hollow, like a drum, it is cooked. If it does not sound hollow, return the loaves, upside-down, to the oven and bake for 5 to 10 minutes.

Kuchen
RICH YEAST CAKE

 ①

A kuchen (koo-khen) *is a traditional*

German yeast cake-bread. It is usually made with a topping — this version uses a streusel topping, although apples, grated chocolate or chopped nuts may be substituted. Serve kuchen as a coffee or tea-time treat.

ONE 2-POUND CAKE

½ oz. yeast
2 tablespoons plus ½ teaspoon sugar
1 tablespoon lukewarm water
8 oz. [2 cups] flour
½ teaspoon salt
¼ teaspoon ground ginger
½ teaspoon grated lemon rind
5 fl. oz. [⅝ cup] lukewarm milk
2 oz. [¼ cup] plus ½ teaspoon
    butter, melted
1 egg, lightly beaten

TOPPING

2 oz. crushed digestive biscuits
    [½ cup crushed graham crackers]
2 tablespoons sugar
1 teaspoon ground cinnamon
2 oz. [¼ cup] butter, softened

Crumble the yeast into a small bowl and mash in the ½ teaspoon of sugar with a fork. Add the water and cream the yeast and water together. Set the bowl aside in

Kuchen, a yeast cake from Germany, is ideal for a mid-morning snack when buttered and served with coffee.

a warm, draught-free place for 15 to 20 minutes, or until the yeast mixture is puffed up and frothy.

Sift the flour, salt and ginger into a large, warmed mixing bowl. Add the lemon rind and remaining sugar and mix well with a wooden spoon. Make a well in the centre and pour in the yeast mixture, the milk, 2 ounces [¼ cup] of melted butter and the egg.

Using your fingers or a spatula, gradually draw the flour mixture into the liquids. Continue mixing until all the flour is incorporated and the dough comes away from the sides of the bowl.

Turn the dough out on to a lightly floured board or marble slab and knead it for 2 to 3 minutes, or until the dough is smooth and elastic. Reflour the surface if the dough becomes sticky.

Rinse, thoroughly dry and lightly grease the large mixing bowl. Shape the dough into a ball and return it to the bowl. Cover the bowl with a clean, damp cloth and set it in a warm, draught-free place. Leave it for 1 to 1½ hours, or until the dough has risen and has almost doubled in bulk.

Lightly grease a 2-pound loaf tin with the remaining ½ teaspoon of butter. Set aside.

Turn the risen dough out of the bowl on to a floured surface and knead it for about 3 minutes. Set it aside for 10

minutes. With a rolling pin, roll out the dough to a square about 1-inch thick. With your hands, shape the dough into a rectangle about 2 inches thick and place it in the loaf tin. Set aside.

Preheat the oven to moderate 350°F (Gas Mark 4, 180°C).

To make the streusel topping, in a medium-sized mixing bowl, combine the crushed biscuits [crackers], sugar, cinnamon and softened butter together with a fork or a wooden spoon. Stir until the mixture resembles fine breadcrumbs. Sprinkle the topping over the dough. Set the tin aside in a warm, draught-free place for 30 minutes, or until the dough has risen.

Place the loaf tin in the centre of the oven and bake for 40 to 45 minutes, or until the kuchen is well risen and the topping is golden brown and slightly crunchy.

Remove the tin from the oven and run a sharp knife around the edge of the kuchen. Carefully slide the kuchen on to a wire rack to cool.

Malt Bread

☆   ①   ⋈ ⋈ ⋈

This delicious bread is best served a day after it is made when the flavour has had time to mature. Serve it in slices with butter.

TWO 1-POUND LOAVES

1 oz. [2 tablespoons] plus 2 teaspoons
   butter
1 oz. fresh yeast
½ teaspoon sugar
5 fl. oz. [⅝ cup] plus 3 tablespoons
   lukewarm water
3 tablespoons malt extract
2 tablespoons black treacle
   [molasses]
1 lb. [4 cups] flour
1 teaspoon salt
8 oz. [1⅓ cups] sultanas or seedless
   raisins

Using the 2 teaspoons of butter, grease
two 1-pound loaf tins. Set aside.

Crumble the yeast into a small bowl
and mash in the sugar with a kitchen fork.
Add 3 tablespoons of the water and cream
the mixture well. Set the bowl aside in a
warm, draught-free place for 15 to 20
minutes or until the yeast mixture is
puffed up and frothy.

In a small saucepan, melt the remaining
butter with the malt extract and treacle
[molasses] over low heat. Remove the pan
from the heat and set aside to cool.

*Scrumptious Malt Bread may be
served toasted for an unusual breakfast, or fresh with jam for tea.*

Sift the flour and salt into a warmed,
large mixing bowl. Make a well in the
centre and pour in the yeast mixture, the
remaining water and the malt mixture.
Using your fingers or a spatula, gradually
draw the flour mixture into the liquids.
Add the sultanas or seedless raisins and
continue mixing until all the flour is
incorporated and the dough comes away
from the sides of the bowl.

Turn the dough out on to a lightly
floured board or marble slab and knead it
for 10 minutes, reflouring the surface if
the dough becomes sticky. The dough
should be elastic and smooth.

Rinse, thoroughly dry and lightly
grease the large mixing bowl. Shape the
dough into a ball and return it to the bowl.
Cover the bowl with a clean damp cloth
and set it aside in a warm, draught-free
place for 1½ hours, or until the dough has
risen and almost doubled in bulk.

Turn the risen dough out of the bowl

on to a floured surface and knead it gently
for 4 minutes. Divide the dough in half
and shape each half into a neat loaf shape.
Place the loaves in the two loaf tins and
return them to a warm place for 45
minutes or until the dough has risen to
the top of the tins.

Preheat the oven to very hot 450°F (Gas
Mark 8, 230°C).

Place the loaf tins in the centre of the
oven and bake for 30 to 40 minutes or
until the bread is well risen and the loaves
shrink slightly from the sides of the tins.

After removing the bread from the
oven, tip the loaves out of the tins and rap
the undersides with your knuckles. If the
bread sounds hollow, like a drum, it is
cooked. If it does not sound hollow, return
the loaf, upside-down, to the oven and
bake for a further 5 minutes.

Cool the loaves on a wire rack.

Hutzelbrot
GERMAN DRIED FRUIT BREAD

Meaning literally 'dried fruit bread',

Hutzelbrot (hoot-zell-braht) *is packed with fruit and nuts. This large quantity of dough requires enormous mixing bowls and baking sheets, so if you do not own 'larger than life mixing utensils', halve the quantity.*

THREE 2-POUND LOAVES

4 oz. [½ cup] plus 1 teaspoon butter, melted
1 oz. fresh yeast
4 oz. [½ cup] plus ½ teaspoon sugar
1 pint 8 fl. oz. [3½ cups] lukewarm water
3 lb. [12 cups] flour
½ teaspoon ground coriander
¼ teaspoon ground fennel seeds
⅛ teaspoons ground cloves
1 teaspoon salt
2 oz [⅓ cup] dried apricots, chopped
2 oz. [⅓ cup] dried pears, chopped
2 oz. [⅓ cup] dried apples, chopped
10 oz. [2 cups] whole hazelnuts
6 oz. [1 cup] seedless raisins
4 oz. [⅔ cup] chopped candied peel

Using the teaspoon of butter, lightly grease three large baking sheets and set them aside.

Crumble the yeast into a small bowl and, with a fork, mash in the ½ teaspoon of sugar. Add 4 fluid ounces [½ cup] of the warm water and cream the water, sugar and yeast together. Set the bowl aside in a warm, draught-free place for 15 to 20 minutes, or until the yeast mixture has risen and is frothy.

Sift half the flour into a large mixing bowl and add the coriander, fennel, cloves and salt. Make a well in the centre of the mixture and pour in the yeast mixture, the remaining melted butter, and the remaining water.

Using your fingers, gradually draw the flour into the liquid. Continue mixing until all the flour is incorporated.

Set the bowl aside for 15 minutes.

Sift the remaining flour into a large mixing bowl and add the chopped dried fruit, hazelnuts, raisins and candied peel. Using your hands mix the flour, fruit and nut mixture into the yeast mixture and turn the dough out on to a floured board or marble slab. Knead the dough well until it is smooth and elastic.

Rinse, thoroughly dry and lightly grease the mixing bowl. With your hands, shape the dough into a ball and return it to the bowl.

Dust the top of the dough with a little flour and cover the bowl with a clean, damp cloth. Set the bowl aside in a warm, draught-free place and leave it for 1 to 1½ hours, or until the dough has risen and almost doubled in bulk.

Turn the risen dough out of the bowl on to a floured surface and knead the dough for 2 minutes.

Using a sharp knife, cut the dough into 3 equal pieces. Shape each piece into a ball.

Place the balls on the baking sheets, cover them with a damp cloth and return them to a warm place for about 30 to 40 minutes, or until they have risen and almost doubled in bulk.

Preheat the oven to hot 425°F (Gas Mark 7, 220°C). When the second rising is completed, place the baking sheets in the oven and bake for 15 minutes. Reduce the oven temperature to fairly hot 375°F (Gas Mark 5, 190°C) and continue baking for 30 minutes or until the tops of the loaves are crusty and golden brown.

After removing the bread from the oven, tip the loaves off the baking sheets and rap the undersides with your knuckles. If the bread sounds hollow, like a drum, it is cooked. If it does not sound hollow, lower the oven temperature to cool 300°F (Gas Mark 2, 150°C), return the loaves on the baking sheets, to the oven and bake them for a further 5 to 10 minutes.

Remove the baking sheets from the oven and cool the loaves on a wire rack.

Hutzelbrot is a delicious German bread made from dried apricots, pears, apples, hazelnuts and raisins.

Coffee Bread

Swedish bread baked in a decorative braid shape and topped with crunchy chopped almonds, Coffee Bread, spread with butter, makes a marvellous coffee snack, or children's home-from-school treat.

4 LOAVES

¾ oz. fresh yeast
8 oz. [1 cup] sugar
1 pint [2½ cups] lukewarm milk
½ teaspoon salt
2 oz. [¼ cup] plus 1 tablespoon butter, melted
2 teaspoons ground cardamom
3 lb. [12 cups] flour

TOPPING

2 eggs, lightly beaten
2 oz. [¼ cup] sugar
3 oz. [¾ cup] chopped almonds

Crumble the yeast into a small bowl. Add 1 teaspoon of the sugar and 1 tablespoon of the milk. With a kitchen fork, cream the yeast, sugar and milk together to make a smooth paste. Set the bowl aside in a warm, draught-free place for 20 minutes or until the yeast mixture is puffed up and frothy.

In a large mixing bowl, combine the remaining milk, sugar, salt, 2 ounces [¼ cup] melted butter, cardamom and 2 tablespoons flour together, beating with a wooden spoon until all the ingredients have blended. Add the yeast paste and stir until it dissolves in the mixture. Reserve 1 tablespoon of the remaining flour and beat the rest into the mixture, stirring briskly until a smooth and firm dough is formed. Sprinkle the remaining tablespoon of flour on top of the dough. Cover the bowl with a clean cloth and place it in a warm, draught-free place for 1½ to 2 hours, or until the dough has doubled in bulk.

Lightly flour a baking board and turn out the risen dough on to it. Knead the dough for 5 minutes, or until it is smooth. Divide the dough into four pieces.

To make one loaf, divide each quarter into three equal pieces. Using your hands, form each piece into a long rope shape. Press the ropes together at one end and plait [braid] them, joining the ropes again at the other end. Repeat this process until all 4 loaves have been formed. Set them aside on a flat surface, cover them with a clean cloth and place them in a warm, draught-free place for a further 1½ hours, or until the bread has doubled in bulk.

Preheat the oven to 375°F (Gas Mark 5, 190°C). Lightly grease 2 large baking sheets with the remaining butter.

Remove the cloth from the loaves and transfer them to the baking sheet. Using a pastry brush, coat each loaf thoroughly with the beaten egg. Sprinkle the top of each loaf with sugar and chopped almonds.

Bake in the centre or upper part of the oven for 20 minutes, or until the loaves are rich golden in colour. Remove from the oven and transfer to a rack to cool.

Bremer Küchen

BREMEN SWEET BREAD

Bremer Kucher (bray-mer KOO-khen) *is a delicious yeast bread with fruit and nuts. It is traditionally made during the Christmas season in Bremen, West Germany, and is served with coffee in all the* konditoreien, *coffee houses, there.*

2 LOAVES

4 oz. [½ cup] plus 1 teaspoon butter
2 oz. yeast
4 oz. [½ cup] plus ½ teaspoon sugar
4 fl. oz. [½ cup] lukewarm water
1 pint plus 6 fl. oz. [3¾ cups] milk
3 lb. [12 cups] flour
1 teaspoon salt
½ teaspoon ground cardamom

grated rind of 3 lemons
6 oz. [1¼ cups] seedless raisins
2 oz. [½ cup] currants
2 oz. sultanas [½ cup raisins]
4 oz. [1 cup] slivered blanched
   almonds
2 tablespoons butter, melted

Grease 2 medium-sized baking sheets with 1 teaspoon butter, using ½ teaspoon of butter for each sheet. Set the greased sheets aside.

Crumble the yeast into a small bowl and with a fork mash in ½ teaspoon of the sugar. Add the warm water and cream the water, sugar and yeast together until the yeast is dissolved. Set the bowl aside in a warm, draught-free place for 20 minutes, or until the yeast has risen and is frothy.

Pour the milk into a small saucepan and over moderately high heat bring it to just under boiling point. Reduce the heat to low and add the remaining butter. When the butter has melted, remove the pan from the heat and allow the milk to cool to lukewarm.

Put the flour, the remaining sugar, salt, ground cardamom and grated lemon rind into a warmed large mixing bowl. Make a well in the centre of the flour mixture and pour in the yeast-and-milk mixture. Using your fingers gradually draw the flour into the liquid. Continue mixing until all the flour is incorporated and the dough comes away from the sides of the bowl.

Turn the dough out on to a floured board or marble slab and knead the dough for about 10 minutes, reflouring the surface if the dough becomes sticky. The dough should then be elastic and smooth.

Rinse, thoroughly dry and lightly grease the large mixing bowl. With your hands shape the dough into a ball and return it to the bowl. Dust the top of the dough with a little flour and cover the bowl with a clean, damp cloth. Set the bowl in a warm, draught-free place and leave it for 1 to 1½ hours, or until the dough has risen and has almost doubled in bulk.

Turn the risen dough out of the bowl on to a floured surface and knead the dough for 2 minutes. Sprinkle the raisins, currants, sultanas and half of the almonds on to the dough, a handful at a time, and knead them in thoroughly until the fruit and nuts are well distributed in the dough.

Using a sharp knife, cut the dough into

A German yeast bread rich with fruit and nuts, Bremer Küchen is delicious served with morning coffee.

2 pieces. Shape each piece into a long loaf. Place the loaves on the baking sheets, cover them with a damp cloth and return them to a warm place for about 30 to 45 minutes, or until they have risen and expanded across the baking sheets.

Preheat the oven to fairly hot 375°F (Gas Mark 5, 190°C).

When the second rising is completed, press the remaining almonds into the top of the dough. Place the baking sheets in the centre of the oven and bake the loaves for 1 hour, or until the tops of the loaves are crusty and golden brown.

After removing the bread from the oven, tip the loaves off the baking sheets and rap the undersides with your knuckles. If the bread sounds hollow, like a drum, it is cooked. If it does not sound hollow, lower the oven temperature to cool 300°F (Gas Mark 2, 150°C), return the loaves, on the baking sheets, to the oven and bake them for a further 5 to 10 minutes.

Remove the baking sheets from the oven and, while the bread is still hot, brush the tops with melted butter. If you prefer, the tops may be dusted with icing [confectioners'] sugar. Allow the bread to cool before serving.

Gingerbread

☆   ①   ✂ ✂

Gingerbread has long been a traditional English tea-bread. Until the nineteenth century, Gingerbread, made in the shape of men and animals, were sold at country fairs. They were covered in gilt paper, and this gave rise to the expression: 'to take the gilt off the gingerbread'.

ONE 2-POUND BREAD
3 oz. [⅜ cup] plus 1 teaspoon butter
8 oz. [2 cups] flour

½ teaspoon bicarbonate of soda
   [baking soda]
1½ teaspoons ground ginger
¼ teaspoon ground cloves
½ teaspoon ground cinnamon
¼ teaspoon salt
4 oz. [½ cup] sugar
1 egg
6 fl. oz. treacle [¾ cup molasses]
8 fl. oz. [1 cup] sour cream
2 oz. [⅓ cup] raisins

Preheat the oven to moderate 350°F (Gas Mark 4, 180°C). Lightly grease a 9½- x 5½- x 2½-inch loaf tin with the teaspoon of butter. Set aside.

Sift the flour, soda, ginger, cloves, cinnamon and salt into a medium-sized mixing bowl. Set aside.

In a large mixing bowl, cream the remaining butter and the sugar together with a wooden spoon until the mixture is light and fluffy. Add the egg and treacle [molasses] and beat until the mixture is smooth. Stir in the sour cream.

Gradually incorporate the flour mixture into the butter-and-sugar mixture, beating constantly until the mixture is smooth. Stir in the raisins.

Pour the mixture into the greased loaf tin and place the tin in the oven. Bake the gingerbread for 1¼ hours, or until a skewer inserted into the centre of the bread comes out clean.

Remove the gingerbread from the oven and allow it to cool a little in the tin. Run the tip of a sharp knife lightly around the edge of the gingerbread and gently ease it out of the tin on to a wire cake rack.

Serve the gingerbread warm or cold.

Ideal to take on a summer picnic Gingerbread has a distinct and refreshing flavour.

For Croissants, cut each pastry square diagonally in half.

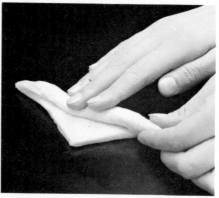
Starting at the base, roll up each triangle and seal the tops with egg.

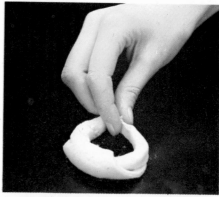
Form the roll into a crescent shape and lightly join the ends together.

Croissants

Croissants (kwa-sawn) are crescent-shaped rolls made of puff pastry or a special croissant paste.

The croissant originated in Budapest in 1686, when the city was besieged by the Turks. Bakers working at night heard the Turks tunnelling beneath the walls and raised the alarm. The Turks were defeated and the bakers were rewarded with the privilege of making pastries in the form of the crescent, the symbol of the Ottoman Empire.

18 CROISSANTS

1 oz. fresh yeast
2 tablespoons plus 1 teaspoon sugar
8 fl. oz. [1 cup] milk
1¼ lb. [5 cups] flour
1 teaspoon salt
10 oz. [1¼ cups] butter, chilled
2 eggs, lightly beaten
GLAZE
1 egg, lightly beaten

Crumble the yeast into a small bowl and mash in the 1 teaspoon sugar with a kitchen fork. Add 2 or 3 tablespoons of the milk and cream the milk and yeast together until the yeast has dissolved. Set the bowl aside in a warm draught-free place for 15 to 20 minutes, or until the yeast mixture has risen and is puffed up and frothy.

Sift 1 pound [4 cups] of the flour, the 2 tablespoons of sugar and the salt into a warmed medium-sized mixing bowl. Add 2 ounces [¼ cup] of the butter and with a knife, cut it into small pieces. With your fingertips rub the butter into the flour until the mixture resembles fine bread-crumbs. Make a well in the centre of the flour mixture and pour in the yeast mixture, the remaining milk and the eggs. Using your fingers or a spatula, gradually draw the flour into the liquid. Continue mixing until all the flour is incorporated and a soft sticky dough is formed.

Dust the top of the dough with a little flour and cover the bowl with a clean cloth. Set the bowl in the refrigerator to chill for 1 hour.

Place the remaining 8 ounces [1 cup] of butter between two pieces of greaseproof or waxed paper. With a rolling pin, roll out the butter into an oblong approximately 9 x 5-inches. Leave the butter wrapped in the paper and place it in the refrigerator.

Sift the remaining flour on to a board or marble slab and turn out the dough on to the flour. Knead the dough for about 10 minutes, or until all the flour on the board or slab has been worked in. The dough should be elastic and smooth.

With a rolling pin, roll out the dough into an oblong about 12 x 8-inches. Unwrap the butter and place it in the centre of the dough. Fold over all four edges of the dough to completely enclose the butter. Roll the dough lengthways into a strip about 15-inches long. Fold the bottom third up to the centre and the top third down. Wrap the folded dough in greaseproof or waxed paper and place it in the refrigerator to chill for 10 minutes. Repeat the rolling out and folding of the dough three more times. Place it in the refrigerator to chill for 10 minutes between each rolling.

After the final rolling leave the dough in the refrigerator to chill for 1 hour.

Sprinkle three baking sheets with a little cold water.

Place the dough on a floured board or marble slab and roll it out into a square ¼-inch thick. Cut the dough first into 5-inch squares and then cut the squares in half diagonally to make triangles.

To shape the croissants, roll the triangles beginning at the base. Brush the tops with a little beaten egg to seal the edge. Form the roll into a crescent shape and join the ends lightly together.

Place the croissants on the dampened baking sheets and leave them in a warm place for 20 to 30 minutes, or until they have doubled in bulk.

Preheat the oven to hot 425°F (Gas Mark 7, 220°C).

Separate the lightly joined ends of the croissants and with a pastry brush, brush the tops with the beaten egg. Bake the croissants in the oven for 15 minutes, or until they are golden brown.

Breakfast Buns

These hot Breakfast Buns sprinkled with sugar and cinnamon are very simple to make. They can be prepared before you start to cook the rest of the breakfast.

12 BUNS

4 tablespoons butter
2 tablespoons vegetable fat
8 oz. [1 cup] sugar
1 egg
8 oz. [2 cups] flour
1½ teaspoons baking powder
½ teaspoon salt
¼ teaspoon ground nutmeg
4 fl. oz. [½ cup] milk
3 oz. [⅜ cup] melted butter
1 teaspoon powdered cinnamon

Preheat the oven to moderate 350°F (Gas Mark 4, 180°C).

Grease 12 cake patty tins with 1 tablespoon of butter. Set the greased tins aside.

In a medium-sized mixing bowl, beat together the remaining butter, the vegetable fat, half of the sugar and the egg with a wooden spoon or rotary beater until the mixture is smooth and creamy.

Sift together the flour, baking powder, salt and nutmeg into another bowl. Beat the flour mixture and the milk into the egg-and-fat mixture.

Spoon the mixture into the greased

Sprinkled with sugar and cinnamon, these hot Breakfast Buns are very popular in the United States.

patty tins, filling them two-thirds full. Place the tins in the oven and bake for 25 minutes, or until the buns are a light brown.

Remove the tins from the oven and, with a palette knife, ease the buns out of the tins on to a wire rack. Brush the buns with the melted butter and sprinkle them with the remaining sugar and cinnamon.

Serve hot.

Baps

Soft, white, Scottish breakfast rolls, baps are delicious served hot with butter. They are simple to prepare, but they cannot be made in a hurry. Though baps are best served hot from the oven, they can be kept a short while and reheated.

8 ROLLS

1 lb. [4 cups] flour

Hot Scottish Baps, split and buttered, are traditionally eaten at breakfast.

½ teaspoon salt
5 fl. oz. plus 2 tablespoons milk
5 fl. oz. water
1 teaspoon sugar
1 tablespoon dried yeast
4 tablespoons butter

Sift the flour and salt into a large mixing bowl. Put in a warm place.

Warm the milk and water, place in a bowl and add the sugar. Sprinkle the yeast on top. Leave in a warm place for 15 minutes or until it is frothy.

Rub the butter into the warm flour-and-salt mixture. Make a well in the middle of the flour and pour in the frothy yeast mixture. With your hands, mix into a soft dough, adding 1 or 2 teaspoons more warm water if necessary.

Place the dough in a greased bowl, cover with a clean cloth and leave it to stand in a warm place for 1 hour or more until it doubles in size.

Preheat the oven to hot 425°F (Gas Mark 7, 220°C).

Grease a baking tin with a little butter and dust with flour. Remove the risen dough from the bowl and knead it on a floured surface. Divide it into 8 equal pieces. Knead each piece separately and pat it into an oval shape. Flatten each piece, place on the baking tin and leave in a warm place for 15 minutes.

Brush each bap with the remaining milk and bake in the oven for 15 to 20 minutes. Serve hot with butter.

Muffin

The muffin has various meanings in different countries.

In North America, it is a breakfast cake made with flour, milk and butter with baking powder used as a raising agent rather than yeast. It is baked in a special pan called a muffin pan.

In Great Britain, on the other hand, the muffin is a teacake made with yeast. It is cooked in a special ring called a muffin ring on top of the stove on a girdle or heavy baking sheet. It is cooked on both sides — unlike the CRUMPET which is made in the same way but is only cooked on one side. To add to the confusion, a popular crumpet-like breakfast cake in the United States is called a muffin!

Muffins with Apples

These fruit muffins, traditional American favourites, are equally delicious eaten warm or cold and are usually served at breakfast. In this particular recipe we use apples but almost any kind of fruit can be substituted.

12 MUFFINS

2 oz. [¼ cup] plus 1 tablespoon butter, melted
8 oz. [2 cups] flour
½ teaspoon salt
2 teaspoons baking powder
2 oz. [¼ cup] sugar
½ teaspoon ground cinnamon
¼ teaspoon grated nutmeg
¼ teaspoon mixed spice or ground allspice
2 eggs, lightly beaten
5 fl. oz. [⅝ cup] buttermilk
1 tablespoon lemon juice
2 medium-sized eating apples, peeled, cored and grated

Preheat the oven to very hot 450°F (Gas Mark 8, 230°C). With the tablespoon of butter, generously grease a 12-muffin pan and set aside.

Sift the flour, salt, baking powder, sugar, cinnamon, nutmeg and mixed spice or ground allspice into a large mixing bowl. Set aside.

In a medium-sized mixing bowl, beat the eggs with a wire whisk or rotary beater until they are pale yellow in colour and fall in a steady ribbon from the whisk. Add the remaining butter, the buttermilk and lemon juice to the eggs and stir well.

Stir the egg mixture into the flour mixture as quickly as possible. Do not over-mix as the ingredients should be just combined. Fold in the grated apples.

Spoon the batter into the prepared muffin pan. Place the pan in the centre of the oven and bake for 15 to 20 minutes or until a skewer inserted into the centres of the muffins comes out clean.

Remove the muffins from the oven. Cool in the pan for about 4 minutes and then turn them out on to a plate, if you are serving them warm.

Muffins with Cheese

Muffins with Cheese make a delightfully different breakfast or brunch addition, served warm, split open and buttered. Place a tomato slice on each muffin for added flavour.

12 MUFFINS

2 oz. [¼ cup] plus 1 tablespoon butter, melted
8 oz. [2 cups] flour
2 teaspoons baking powder
½ teaspoon salt
⅛ teaspoon black pepper
2 eggs
5 fl. oz. [⅝ cup] milk
2 oz. [½ cup] Cheddar cheese, grated

A delightful way to begin your day, Muffins with Apples make a tasty change from toast at breakfast-time.

Preheat the oven to very hot 450°F (Gas Mark 8, 230°C). With the tablespoon of butter, generously grease a 12-muffin pan and set aside.

Sift the flour, baking powder, salt and pepper into a large mixing bowl. Set aside.

In a medium-sized mixing bowl, beat the eggs with a wire whisk or rotary beater until they are pale yellow in colour and fall in a steady ribbon from the whisk. Add the remaining butter and the milk to the eggs and stir well.

Stir the egg mixture into the flour mixture as quickly as possible. Do not over-mix as the ingredients should be just combined. Stir in the grated cheese.

Spoon the batter into the prepared muffin pan. Place the pan in the centre of the oven and bake for 15 to 20 minutes or until a skewer inserted into the centres of the muffins comes out clean.

Remove the muffins from the oven. Cool in the pan for about 4 minutes and then turn them out on to a plate, if you are serving them warm.

Muffins with Herbs

Lightly flavoured with herbs and a hint of

orange, Muffins with Herbs make an unusual breakfast treat. Serve warm, with butter.

36 MUFFINS

4 oz. [½ cup] plus 2 tablespoons butter, melted

14 oz. [3½ cups] flour

1 teaspoon salt

4 teaspoons baking powder

2 tablespoons very finely chopped fresh parsley

½ teaspoon dried marjoram

½ teaspoon ground coriander

¼ teaspoon mixed spice or ground allspice

⅛ teaspoon black pepper grated rind of 1 orange

4 eggs

10 fl. oz. [1¼ cups] buttermilk

Preheat the oven to very hot 450°F (Gas Mark 8, 230°C). With the 2 tablespoons of butter, generously grease three 12-muffin pans and set them aside.

Sift the flour, salt and baking powder into a large mixing bowl. Stir in the parsley, marjoram, coriander, mixed spice or ground allspice, black pepper and orange rind. Set aside.

In a medium-sized mixing bowl, beat the eggs with a wire whisk or rotary beater until they are pale yellow in colour and fall in a steady ribbon from the whisk.

Just for a change, try light and aromatic Muffins with Herbs.

Add the remaining butter and the buttermilk to the eggs and stir well.

Stir the egg mixture into the flour mixture as quickly as possible. Do not overmix as the ingredients should be just combined.

Spoon the batter into the prepared muffin pans. Place the pans in the centre of the oven and bake for 15 to 20 minutes or until a skewer inserted into the centres of the muffins comes out clean.

Remove the muffins from the oven. Cool in the pans for about 4 minutes and then turn them out on to a plate. Serve warm.

Buttermilk Scones

These American scones are easy-to-make. The addition of buttermilk to the batter makes them especially light and fluffy. They are ideal to serve for tea with butter and jam.

18 SCONES

2 oz. [¼ cup] plus ½ tablespoon butter

12 oz. [3 cups] flour

1 teaspoon salt

1 teaspoon baking powder

½ teaspoon bicarbonate of soda [baking soda]

10 fl. oz. [1¼ cups] commercial buttermilk

Preheat the oven to hot 425°F (Gas Mark 7, 220°C). Grease a baking sheet with ½ tablespoon of the butter.

Sift the flour, salt, baking powder and soda into a medium-sized mixing bowl. With your fingertips, rub the remaining butter into the flour mixture until the mixture resembles coarse bread-crumbs. Using a fork, stir in enough buttermilk to make a soft dough.

Turn the dough out on to a lightly floured board. Knead it gently for 30 seconds. Roll out the dough to ½-inch thickness. With a 2-inch round pastry cutter, cut out the scones and place them on the prepared baking sheet.

Bake the scones in the oven for 15 minutes, or until a skewer inserted in one of the scones comes out clean. Serve hot or cool.

Baking Powder Biscuits

An American recipe, Baking Powder Biscuits are like English scones. They may be served hot with butter for lunch or supper, or with jam for tea.

12 TO 15 BISCUITS

8 oz. [2 cups] flour
2 teaspoons baking powder
1 teaspoon salt
2 tablespoons butter, chilled
2 tablespoons vegetable shortening
5 fl. oz. milk

Preheat the oven to hot 425°F (Gas Mark 7, 220°C).

Sift the flour, baking powder and salt into a medium-sized mixing bowl. Add the butter and vegetable shortening and cut them into the flour with a table knife. With your fingertips, crumble the fat and flour together. Stir in enough milk to make a soft and light dough. Add a little more milk if the dough is too dry, or more flour if it is too sticky.

Turn the dough on to a floured surface. With floured hands, knead the dough lightly until it is smooth. Roll it out until it is ¾-inch thick. Cut into 2-inch rounds with a pastry cutter.

Place the biscuits on an ungreased baking sheet, prick with a fork and bake for 12 to 15 minutes.

An unusual type of scone, American Baking Powder Biscuits are delicious served hot with butter and jam.

Corn Meal Biscuits

These little golden scones are inexpensive and easy to make. Serve them hot, split open and spread with butter and honey for snacks with coffee, or serve them plain as an accompaniment to soups or stews.

20 BISCUITS

2½ oz. [½ cup] fine-ground corn meal
5½ oz. [1⅜ cups] flour
½ teaspoon salt
2 teaspoons baking powder
2 tablespoons vegetable fat, chilled and cut into small pieces
2 tablespoons butter, chilled and cut into small pieces
4 fl. oz. [½ cup] milk

Preheat the oven to hot 425°F (Gas Mark 7, 220°C).

Sift the corn meal, flour, salt and baking powder into a medium-sized mixing bowl. With your fingertips, rub the fat and butter into the flour mixture until it resembles fine breadcrumbs.

Gradually add the milk to the mixture, stirring with a wooden spoon until the dough is firm and comes away from the sides of the bowl.

Turn the dough out on to a lightly floured board and knead it gently for 2 to 3 minutes, or until it is soft and pliable. Roll the dough into a ball and flatten it

with the palm of your hand. Using a lightly floured rolling pin, roll the dough into a circle ½-inch to ¾-inch thick. With a 2 inch pastry cutter, cut the dough into rounds. Arrange the rounds, fairly close together, on an ungreased baking sheet and place on the top shelf of the oven.

Bake for 15 minutes, or until the tops of the biscuits have browned. Serve immediately or cool on a wire rack.

Pomeroy Rolls

Delightful little yeast rolls in the shape of clover leaves, Pomeroy Rolls have dried apricots, marinated in sweet wine, added to the dough before cooking. Serve warm, with plenty of butter and honey or home-made apricot jam.

24 ROLLS

6 oz. [1 cup] dried apricots, finely chopped
2 fl. oz. [¼ cup] lukewarm sweet white wine
½ oz. fresh yeast
2 oz. [¼ cup] plus ½ teaspoon sugar
10 fl. oz. [1¼ cups] lukewarm milk
1 lb. [4 cups] flour
1 teaspoon salt
3 oz. [⅜ cup] plus 2 teaspoons butter, melted

Place the apricots in a small bowl and pour over the wine. Set aside to marinate for 30 minutes. Drain the apricots and reserve the wine.

Meanwhile, crumble the yeast into a small bowl and mash in the ½ teaspoon of sugar with a fork. Add 2 fluid ounces [¼ cup] of the milk and cream the milk and yeast together. Set the bowl aside in a warm, draught-free place for 15 to 20 minutes or until the yeast mixture is puffed up and frothy.

Sift the flour, the remaining sugar and the salt into a warmed, large mixing bowl. Make a well in the centre and pour in the reserved wine, yeast mixture, the remaining milk and 2 ounces [¼ cup] of the butter. Using your fingers or a spatula, gradually draw the flour mixture into the liquids. Continue mixing until all the flour is incorporated and the dough comes away from the sides of the bowl.

Turn the dough out on to a lightly floured board or marble slab and knead it for 10 minutes, reflouring the surface if the dough becomes sticky. The dough should be elastic and smooth.

Rinse, thoroughly dry and lightly grease the large mixing bowl. Shape the dough into a ball and return it to the bowl. Cover the bowl with a clean, damp cloth and set it in a warm, draught-free

Little clover leaf-shaped rolls filled with dried apricots marinated in wine, Pomeroy Rolls should be served warm with lots of butter and honey or home-made apricot jam.

place for 1 to 1½ hours, or until the dough has risen and has almost doubled in bulk.

Using the 2 teaspoons of butter, grease 24 patty tins. Set aside.

Turn the risen dough out of the bowl on to a floured surface. Roll the dough out slightly and sprinkle with the apricots. Press the apricots into the dough and knead it for 8 minutes. Make 72 very small balls by rolling pieces of the dough between the palms of your hands. Place 3 balls into each patty tin and return the tins to a warm, draught-free place for 45 minutes to 1 hour or until the dough has almost doubled in bulk and risen to the tops of the tins.

Preheat the oven to hot 425°F (Gas Mark 7, 220°C).

Using a pastry brush, brush the dough with the remaining melted butter. Place the tins in the oven and bake for 15 to 20 minutes or until the rolls are golden brown.

Remove the tins from the oven. Turn the rolls out on to a wire rack to cool before serving.

Raisin Rolls

☆ ☆   ①   ⋈ ⋈ ⋈

Little rolls of sweet bread, stuffed with raisins and currants, Raisin Rolls are delicious eaten warm. Whilst cooking, the butter and sugar melt together, and literally "fry" the rolls, giving them an unusual crispy coating.

ABOUT 12 ROLLS

½ oz. fresh yeast
2 oz. [¼ cup] plus ½ teaspoon soft brown sugar
10 fl. oz. [1¼ cups] lukewarm milk
1 lb. [4 cups] flour
1 teaspoon salt
¼ teaspoon ground cinnamon
¼ teaspoon ground ginger
4 oz. [½ cup] plus 1 teaspoon butter, softened
4 oz. [⅔ cup] raisins
2 oz. [⅓ cup] currants

Into a small bowl, crumble the yeast and mash in the ½ teaspoon of sugar with a fork. Add 2 fluid ounces [¼ cup] of the milk and cream the milk and yeast mixture together. Set the bowl aside in a warm, draught-free place for 15 to 20 minutes or until the yeast mixture is puffed up and frothy.

Sift the flour, salt, cinnamon and ginger into a warmed, large mixing bowl. Make

a well in the centre and pour in the yeast mixture and the remaining milk. Using your fingers or a spatula, gradually draw the flour mixture into the liquids. Continue mixing until all the flour is incorporated and the dough comes away from the sides of the bowl.

Turn the dough out on to a lightly floured board or marble slab and knead it for 10 minutes, reflouring the surface if the dough becomes sticky. The dough should be elastic and smooth.

Rinse, thoroughly dry and lightly grease the large mixing bowl. Shape the dough into a ball and return it to the bowl. Cover the bowl with a clean, damp cloth and set aside in a warm, draught-free place for 1 to 1½ hours, or until the dough has risen and has almost doubled in bulk.

Meanwhile, using the teaspoon of butter, grease a baking sheet. Set aside.

Turn the risen dough out of the bowl on to a lightly floured surface and knead for 4 minutes. Roll the dough out into an oblong about ½-inch thick. Using a table knife, spread the remaining butter over the dough. Sprinkle over the remaining sugar, the raisins and currants.

Roll up the dough tightly, Swiss [jelly] roll style. With a sharp knife, cut the roll into 1-inch wide slices. Lay the slices, ½-inch apart, on the baking sheet.

Preheat the oven to hot 425°F (Gas Mark 7, 220°C).

Set the baking sheet aside in a warm draught free place for 20 minutes or until the dough slices have almost doubled in size. Place the baking sheet in the oven and bake the rolls for 15 minutes.

Remove the baking sheet from the oven. With the help of a fish slice, turn each roll over. Return the baking sheet to the oven and continue to bake for a further 10 minutes or until the rolls are well risen and golden brown.

Remove the baking sheet from the oven and transfer the rolls to a wire rack. Allow the rolls to cool for 10 minutes, if you are serving them warm, or allow to cool completely before serving.

Devonshire Splits

☆   ①   ⋈ ⋈ ⋈

These mouth-watering yeast buns are traditionally split in half and spread with thick Devonshire cream and strawberry jam. They may be served either hot or cold.

16 BUNS

½ oz. fresh yeast
1 teaspoon castor sugar
2 tablespoons lukewarm water
1 lb. [4 cups] flour
¼ teaspoon salt

Crispy, sweet Raisin Rolls, flavoured with spices — eat them warm from the oven, or cold with butter.

---

10 fl. oz. [1¼ cups] lukewarm milk
2 tablespoons melted butter

In a small mixing bowl, cream the yeast and sugar together. Stir in the lukewarm water and set the bowl aside in a warm, draught-free place for 15 to 20 minutes, or until the yeast mixture is puffed up and frothy.

Sift the flour and salt into a large mixing bowl. Make a well in the centre and pour in the yeast mixture, the milk and the melted butter. Mix the liquid ingredients into the flour with your hands or a spoon until it forms a soft dough. Turn the dough out on to a floured board or marble surface and knead it for 5 minutes.

Put the dough in a greased bowl. Cover with a clean cloth, or put the bowl in a polythene bag, and leave it in a warm, draught-free place for 1½ hours, or until the dough has doubled in bulk.

Turn the dough out on to the floured board and knead it gently for 1 to 2 minutes.

Preheat the oven to hot 425°F (Gas Mark 7, 220°C).

Form the dough into 16 round balls. Place the balls on a floured baking sheet. Leave them for 20 minutes in a warm, draught-free place.

Place the buns in the oven and bake

them for 15 minutes. Serve either hot or cold.

A real treat for tea, Devonshire Splits are mouth-watering yeast buns. Serve with cream and strawberry jam.

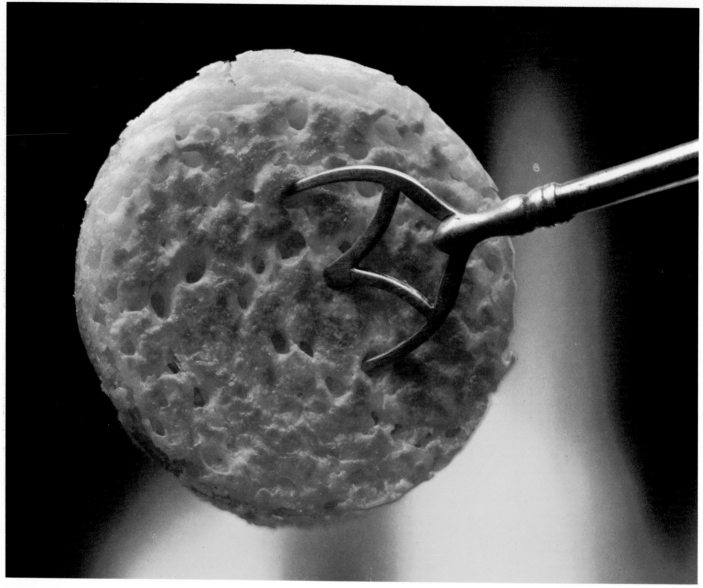

Crumpet

A crumpet is a type of English tea-cake made of milk, flour, yeast and salt, which is known as an English muffin in the United States. It has a spongy texture, filled with holes. Crumpets are toasted, preferably before an open fire, and eaten spread thickly with butter.

Crumpets

☆ ① ✕ ✕

Crumpets are a traditional tea or supper dish, and should ideally be toasted before an open fire, then stacked in a pile with a large knob of butter on top, and the butter allowed to drain slowly through the pile. The crumpets may be eaten simply with butter or with jam or honey. You will need crumpet rings and, if possible, a girdle to cook the crumpets. Otherwise, a baking sheet may be used. A girdle, also known as a griddle, is described at the end of this recipe.

24 CRUMPETS

½ oz. fresh yeast
½ teaspoon sugar
1 pint [2½ cups] milk, warmed
1 lb. [4 cups] flour
½ teaspoon salt
1 egg
3 oz. [⅜ cup] butter, melted

Crumble the yeast into a small mixing bowl. Add the sugar and 2 to 3 table-spoons of the milk. With a fork mash the yeast, sugar and milk to a smooth paste. Set the bowl aside in a warm, draught-free place for 15 to 20 minutes or until the yeast mixture is puffed up and frothy.

Sift the flour and salt into a large warm mixing bowl. Make a well in the centre and pour in the yeast mixture, the remaining milk, the egg and one-third of the melted butter.

Beat the ingredients with a wooden spoon until they form a smooth thin batter. Cover the bowl with a clean cloth and leave it in a warm, draught-free place for 40 to 45 minutes or until the

English Crumpets are toasted and eaten hot, spread thickly with butter.

batter has doubled in volume.

Grease a large girdle or baking sheet and the crumpet rings with half of the remaining melted butter. Put the rings on the girdle or baking sheet and place it over moderate heat. When the rings and girdle or baking sheet are hot, spoon about 2 tablespoons of the batter into each ring to fill it about one-third full. Reduce the heat to moderately low and cook the crumpets for 5 to 6 minutes or until the top surfaces are set and full of holes and the bottoms are golden brown.

Transfer the crumpets to a wire cake rack to cool. Grease the girdle and rings again and cook the remaining crumpets in the same way.

Girdle

A girdle, also known as a griddle, is a round, flat, heavy iron pan. It either has a half-loop handle or, more commonly in the United States, a long handle.

A girdle is used, mostly in Scotland, Ireland and the North of England, for making scones, pancakes and teacakes.

To use a girdle, it is necessary to rub it first with salt to make sure it is smooth and clean. The salt is then dusted off.

The girdle should be heated until a teaspoon of flour sprinkled over the surface turns brown in 2 minutes.

For scones and teacakes, the girdle should be dredged with flour, but for pancakes, it should be lightly greased with lard or butter.

Scones and teacakes should not be less than ¾-inch thick and they will require cooking for 3 to 5 minutes on each side.

Do not wash the girdle after cooking — it should just be wiped clean and kept in a dry place. If water is left on the surface it will rust.

Bath Buns

Made with eggs and yeast and rich with currants and candied peel, these sweet buns were first made in Bath in the eighteenth century when this English spa was at the height of its popularity. Served at tea, they are usually split and buttered.

12 BUNS

3 oz. [⅜ cup] plus 1 teaspoon sugar
5 fl. oz. lukewarm milk
½ oz. fresh yeast
1 lb. [4 cups] flour
½ teaspoon salt
4 oz. [½ cup] butter
2 eggs, lightly beaten
4 oz. [¾ cup] currants
2 oz. [¼ cup] candied peel
½ egg lightly beaten with 1 tablespoon milk and sweetened with 1 tablespoon sugar
2 oz. [¼ cup] sugar

In a small mixing bowl dissolve 1 teaspoon sugar in the warm milk. Crumble the yeast on top and mix well. Leave the milk-and-yeast mixture in a warm place for 15 minutes or until it becomes frothy.

Sift the flour and the salt into a warm mixing bowl and mix in the remaining sugar. With your fingertips rub the butter into the flour mixture.

Make a well in the centre of the flour mixture and pour in the frothy yeast and the beaten eggs. Mix in with a fork and then, using well-floured hands, knead lightly to make a soft dough.

Put the dough in a greased bowl, cover with a cloth or a plastic bag and place in a warm place for 1 hour,

Bath Buns, rich with currants and candied peel, are traditional English tea-time favourites.

or until the dough has doubled in size.

Turn the dough on to a floured board and knead in the currants and candied peel.

Preheat the oven to hot 375°F (Gas Mark 5, 190°C). Lightly grease a baking sheet.

Divide the dough into 12 pieces and shape into buns. Place the buns on the baking sheet, well spaced to leave room for them to rise. Cover them with the cloth or plastic bag and place in a warm place to rise for another 30 minutes.

Brush the top with the sweetened egg and milk mixture and sprinkle with the sugar. Place the buns in the oven and bake for 25 to 30 minutes.

Cumin and Raspberry Buns

These unusual cumin-flavoured buns, with raspberry jam in the centre, are delicious eaten warm or cold.

24 BUNS

6 oz. [¾ cup] plus 1 teaspoon butter
8 oz. [1 cup] plus 2 tablespoons sugar
2 eggs
1 teaspoon ground cumin
12 oz. [3 cups] self-raising flour
⅛ teaspoon salt
4 oz. raspberry jam

Preheat the oven to fairly hot 375°F (Gas Mark 5, 190°C). Grease two cup cake tins with the teaspoon of butter.

Place the remaining butter and 8 ounces [1 cup] of the sugar in a large mixing bowl. Cream them together with a wooden spoon until the mixture is light

Cumin and Raspberry Buns make an unusual teatime treat — children and adults alike will love them.

and fluffy. Beat in the eggs and cumin. Sift in the flour and salt and beat until all the ingredients are thoroughly blended. Place the bowl in the refrigerator and chill the dough for 30 minutes, or until it is very firm and cold.

Roll the dough into small balls, each about the size of a large walnut, and roll each ball in the remaining 2 tablespoons of sugar. With your thumb, make a dent in the centre of each ball. Fill the dent with raspberry jam. Squeeze the dent closed so that the jam is completely covered. Place the balls in the greased cup cake tins and bake in the oven for 20 minutes, or until they have risen and are golden in colour.

Cool the buns on a wire rack.

Maritozzi Uso Fornaio

PINE NUT AND ORANGE BUNS

☆ ① ⋈ ⋈ ⋈

Italian buns flavoured with pine nuts, orange rind and wine-soaked sultanas or raisins, Maritozzi Uso Fornaio (mah-ree-tot-zee oo-soh fohr-ny-yoh) are delicious served for tea, plain or buttered.

8 BUNS

¼ oz. fresh yeast
2 oz. [¼ cup] plus ¼ teaspoon sugar
1 tablespoon lukewarm water
4 fl. oz. [½ cup] milk
2 oz. [¼ cup] butter, cut into small

pieces
12 oz. [3 cups] flour
¼ teaspoon salt
1 egg, lightly beaten
3 oz. [½ cup] sultanas or raisins
2 fl. oz. [¼ cup] sweet white wine
2 teaspoons olive oil
3 tablespoons blanched pine nuts, coarsely chopped
3 oz. [½ cup] finely diced candied orange rind
1 egg yolk, well beaten with 2 tablespoons milk

Crumble the yeast into a small mixing bowl. With a fork, mash in ¼ teaspoon of the sugar. Add the lukewarm water and cream the ingredients together to form a smooth paste. Set aside in a warm, draught-free place for 15 to 20 minutes, or until the yeast mixture is puffed up and frothy.

Meanwhile, pour the milk into a small saucepan and add the butter pieces. Set the pan over moderate heat and scald the milk (bring to just under boiling point), stirring occasionally. Remove the pan from the heat and set it aside to cool to lukewarm

Sift the flour and salt into a medium-sized mixing bowl. Stir in the remaining sugar. Make a well in the centre of the flour mixture and pour in the yeast mixture, the beaten egg and the lukewarm milk and butter mixture. Using your fingers or a spatula, mix the liquids together, gradually drawing in the flour. Continue mixing until all the flour has been incorporated and the dough comes away from the sides of the bowl.

Turn the dough out on to a lightly floured surface. Knead the dough for 10 minutes, or until it is smooth and elastic. Shape the dough into a ball.

Rinse, dry and lightly grease the mixing bowl. Place the ball of dough in the bowl and cover with a clean, damp cloth. Set the bowl aside in a warm, draught-free

Fragrant pine nut and orange buns from Italy, Maritozzi Uso Fornaio may be served plain or buttered.

place for 1 to 1¼ hours, or until the dough has risen and doubled in bulk.

Meanwhile, in a small mixing bowl, combine the sultanas or raisins and the wine. Set aside for 15 minutes, or until the sultanas or raisins are swollen. Drain off any excess wine and lightly pat the fruit dry with kitchen paper towels. Set the fruit aside.

Line a large baking sheet with non-stick silicone paper and set it aside.

Turn the risen dough out on to a lightly floured surface. With the heel of your hand, flatten the dough into an oblong. Using a pastry brush, brush the dough with the olive oil. Sprinkle over the sultanas or raisins, pine nuts and chopped candied orange rind.

Fold the dough over into three and knead it vigorously for 6 to 8 minutes, or until it is smooth and the fruit, nuts and oil are evenly blended into the dough.

Break the dough off into 8 equal pieces and roll the pieces between your hands into balls. Place the balls, well-spaced, on the prepared baking sheet.

Cover the dough with a clean, damp cloth and set aside in a warm, draught-free place for 30 to 40 minutes, or until the balls have risen and almost doubled in bulk.

Preheat the oven to fairly hot 400°F (Gas Mark 6, 200°C).

Using a pastry brush, lightly brush the balls with the egg yolk and milk mixture.

Place the baking sheet in the centre of the oven and bake the buns for 20 to 25 minutes, or until they are golden brown on top.

Remove the baking sheet from the oven. Transfer the buns to a wire rack to cool completely before serving.

Lemon and Walnut Buns

  ①

These fragrant lemon and walnut flavoured buns taste even better split open and spread with butter and jam. Serve them at tea time, or with morning coffee, warm from the oven.
12 BUNS

½ oz. fresh yeast
3 oz. [⅜ cup] plus ½ teaspoon
  sugar
5 fl. oz. [⅝ cup] lukewarm milk
1 lb. [4 cups] flour
⅛ teaspoon salt
¼ teaspoon ground mixed spice or
  allspice
4 oz. [½ cup] butter
2 eggs, well beaten
  finely grated rind of 2 lemons
1 tablespoon lemon juice
4 oz. [⅔ cup] chopped walnuts
2 oz. [⅓ cup] mixed candied peel

Lemon and Walnut Buns can be served plain or with butter and jam for tea.

1 egg yolk well beaten with 2
  tablespoons milk
4 tablespoons brown sugar

Line a large baking sheet with non-stick silicone paper and set it aside.

Crumble the yeast into a small mixing bowl and with a fork mash in ½ teaspoon of the sugar. Add 2 to 3 tablespoons of the milk and cream the mixture. Set it aside in a warm, draught-free place for 15 to 20 minutes, or until the yeast mixture is puffed up and frothy.

Meanwhile, sift the flour, salt and ground mixed spice or allspice into a medium-sized mixing bowl. Stir in the remaining sugar.

Add the butter and cut it into small pieces with a table knife. Using your fingers, rub the butter into the flour.

Make a well in the centre of the flour mixture. Pour in the yeast mixture, the remaining milk, the beaten eggs, lemon rind and juice. Using a spatula or your fingers, mix the liquids together, gradually drawing in the flour.

When all the flour has been incorpor-ated, turn the dough out on to a floured surface. With your hands, knead the dough for 7 to 10 minutes, or until it feels smooth and elastic.

Rinse, dry and lightly grease the mixing bowl. Shape the dough into a ball and place it in the bowl. Sprinkle the top with a little flour. Cover the bowl with a clean, damp cloth and set it aside in a warm, draught-free place for at least 1½ hours, or until the dough has almost doubled in bulk.

Turn the dough out on to a floured surface. With the palms of your hands, flatten the dough into an oblong. Sprinkle over the chopped walnuts and the mixed candied peel. Fold the dough over. Knead it for 6 to 8 minutes, or until the nuts and candied peel are evenly distributed and the dough is smooth.

Divide the dough into 12 equal pieces and shape them into balls.

Place the balls on the prepared baking sheet, cover with a clean damp cloth and set aside in a warm, draught-free place for 30 to 40 minutes, or until they have doubled in bulk.

Preheat the oven to fairly hot 375°F (Gas Mark 5, 190°C).

Using a pastry brush, coat the balls of dough with the egg yolk and milk mixture.

Sprinkle the brown sugar over the tops.

Place the baking sheet in the centre of the oven and bake the buns for 25 to 30 minutes, or until they are cooked and golden brown on top.

Remove the baking sheet from the oven and transfer the buns to a wire rack to cool to room temperature before serving.

London Buns

These quickly made buns make ideal snacks for children. For a slightly different flavour and texture, substitute buttermilk for the milk in this recipe.

8 BUNS

2 oz. [¼ cup] plus 1 teaspoon butter
8 oz. [2 cups] flour
2 teaspoons bicarbonate of soda [baking soda]
1 teaspoon cream of tartar
2 oz. [¼ cup] sugar
4 oz. [⅔ cup] chopped mixed peel
coarsely grated rind of 1 lemon
1 egg yolk
3 fl. oz. [⅜ cup] milk
2 tablespoons crushed nut brittle toffee

Using the teaspoon of butter, grease two baking sheets and set aside.

Sweet, crunchy London Buns, flavoured with mixed peel, are simple to make.

Preheat the oven to fairly hot 400°F (Gas Mark 6, 200°C).

Sift the flour, soda and cream of tartar into a large mixing bowl. Add the butter and cut it into small pieces with a table knife. With your fingertips, rub the fat into the flour until the mixture resembles coarse breadcrumbs. Stir in the sugar, chopped peel and lemon rind. Add the egg yolk and milk and, using a table knife, stir the mixture until it forms large lumps, adding a little more milk if the dough is too dry.

Using your hands, knead the dough lightly. Form the dough into a large firm ball.

Divide the dough into eight equal pieces. Place the crushed nut brittle in a small bowl. Roll the pieces of dough into balls. Dip each ball in the crushed nut brittle. Place the buns on the baking sheets. Put the baking sheets in the oven and bake the buns for 15 minutes, or until they are golden brown.

Remove the buns from the oven, transfer them to a wire rack and leave them to cool completely before serving.

Hot Cross Buns

Hot Cross Buns, a traditional British Easter treat on sale at all the bakeries during the week before Easter, are fragrant fruit buns decorated with a cross, and

eaten toasted and well-buttered.

16 BUNS

½ oz. fresh yeast
2 oz. [¼ cup] plus ¼ teaspoon sugar
8 fl. oz. [1 cup] plus 2 tablespoons lukewarm milk
1 lb. [4 cups] plus 1 tablespoon flour
½ teaspoon salt
1 teaspoon ground mixed spice or allspice
1 teaspoon ground cinnamon
2 eggs
2 oz. [¼ cup] plus 1 tablespoon unsalted butter, melted
2 oz. [⅓ cup] raisins
2 oz. [⅓ cup] chopped mixed candied peel

PASTRY FOR THE CROSSES
1 tablespoon butter
1 oz. [2 tablespoons] flour
1 teaspoon cold water

GLAZE
2 tablespoons milk mixed with 1 teaspoon sugar

Crumble the yeast into a small bowl and mash in the ¼ teaspoon of sugar with a kitchen fork. Add the 2 tablespoons of lukewarm milk and cream the milk and yeast together. Set the bowl aside in a warm draught-free place for 15 to 20 minutes or until the yeast mixture is puffed up and frothy.

Sift the 1 pound [4 cups] of flour, the remaining sugar, the salt, spice and cinnamon into a warmed, large mixing

Decorated with a cross, Hot Cross Buns are traditionally eaten at Easter.

bowl. Make a well in the centre and pour in the yeast mixture, the remaining milk, the eggs and 2 ounces [¼ cup] of the melted butter. Using your fingers or a spatula, gradually draw the flour mixture into the liquids. Continue mixing until all the flour is incorporated and the dough comes away from the sides of the bowl.

Turn the dough out on to a lightly floured board or marble slab and knead it for 10 minutes, re-flouring the surface if the dough becomes sticky. The dough should be elastic and smooth.

Rinse, thoroughly dry and lightly grease the large mixing bowl. Shape the dough into a ball and return it to the bowl. Dust the top of the ball with the tablespoon of flour. Cover the bowl with a clean damp cloth and place it in a warm draught-free place. Leave it for 1 hour or until the dough has risen and almost doubled in bulk.

Punch down the dough and turn it out

of the bowl on to a floured surface. Knead it lightly, working in the raisins and mixed candied peel.

Preheat the oven to very hot 450°F (Gas Mark 8, 230°C).

Divide the dough into 16 equal pieces and shape the pieces into buns.

Grease two baking sheets with the tablespoon of butter. Arrange the buns 2 inches apart on the baking sheets and return them to a warm draught-free place for about 15 to 20 minutes until the buns have almost doubled in bulk.

Meanwhile, make the dough for the crosses. In a small mixing bowl, rub the butter into the flour with your fingertips until the mixture resembles fine breadcrumbs. Mix in the cold water to make a firm dough. On a lightly floured surface, roll out the dough into a rectangle, ⅛-inch thick. Cut the dough into thin strips. Trim the strips and cut them into 2-inch lengths. Press the dough strips into crosses on the tops of the buns.

Brush the buns lightly with the milk and sugar glaze. Place the baking sheets in the centre of the oven and bake the

buns for 15 minutes or until the tops of the buns are deep golden brown.

Remove the baking sheets from the oven and transfer the buns to a wire rack to cool.

Caraway Knots

These popular savoury Knots are delicious served warm with butter or cheese.

20 KNOTS

15 fl. oz. [1⅞ cups] milk
2 oz. [¼ cup] butter
2 lb. [8 cups] plus 1 tablespoon flour
1 tablespoon salt
1 tablespoon sugar
¾ oz. fresh yeast
2 teaspoons lukewarm water
1 egg
3 tablespoons caraway seeds
1 teaspoon vegetable oil
1 egg, lightly beaten

Pour the milk into a small saucepan and place it over low heat to scald the milk

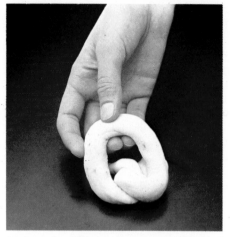

For Caraway Knots, form the ropes of dough into a loop, with crossed ends.

Make a twist at the base of the loop and spread the tips apart.

Bring the loop over to the tips and pinch them to the loop.

(bring it to just under boiling point). Remove the pan from the heat and add the butter. When the butter had melted, set the pan aside and leave the milk to cool to lukewarm.

Sift the 2 pounds [8 cups] of flour, the salt and sugar into a medium-sized mixing bowl.

Crumble the yeast into a small bowl. Add the warm water and mash to a paste with a fork. With a wooden spoon, beat the egg and the yeast paste into the lukewarm milk-and-butter mixture.

Make a well in the centre of the flour

mixture and pour in the yeast-and-milk mixture. Using the wooden spoon or your hands, gradually incorporate the flour into the liquid and continue mixing until a smooth dough is formed.

Fold in 2 tablespoons of caraway seeds. Sprinkle the remaining flour over the dough. Cover the bowl with a cloth and put it in a warm place to rise for 1 to 1½ hours or until the dough has almost doubled in bulk.

Using a pastry brush, lightly grease 2 baking sheets with the oil.

Turn the dough out on to a lightly

floured surface and knead it for about 5 minutes or until it is smooth.

Roll the dough into a 12-inch long roll and with a sharp knife slice it into 20 equal pieces. Roll one slice between your hands to make a thin rope about 14 inches long. Place the rope on a board and shape it into a loop with its ends crossed. Turn the ends of the rope over again to make a twist at the base of the loop. Spread the tips of the two ends apart, bring the loop over to them and pinch the tips to the loop. Do the same with each slice of dough. After all the knots have been formed, leave them to rest for 10 minutes.

Fill a large saucepan two-thirds full with water. Bring the water to the boil over high heat. Lay 2 knots at a time in the water. The knots will sink to the bottom, and then rise to the surface of the water and will double in size.

With a slotted spoon, carefully transfer the knots from the water to the greased baking sheets.

If the knots have come untwisted, gently press them into their original shape.

Leave the knots in a warm place for 15 minutes or until they are almost dry.

Preheat the oven to fairly hot 400°F (Gas Mark 6, 200°C).

Using a pastry brush, coat the knots with the beaten egg and sprinkle them with the rest of the caraway seeds.

Place the knobs in the oven and bake for 15 to 20 minutes, or until they are golden brown. Remove the knots from the oven and, using a palette knife or spatula, transfer them from the trays to a wire cake rack. Serve warm.

Pretzel

A pretzel is a savoury biscuit, twisted into the shape of a loose knot. The dough is glazed with eggs, flavoured with caraway seeds and coarse salt, and baked.

Pretzels originated in Germany, where they have been eaten since Roman times. Many superstitions surround them — for instance, they were supposed, if worn, to have particular efficacy in warding off evil spirits.

Pretzels

☆ ☆   ①   ⋈ ⋈

Pretzels are crisp, crunchy biscuits, delicious served on their own with drinks or, as an alternative to more traditional biscuits, as an accompaniment to cheese. Pretzels may be stored for up to 2 weeks in an airtight tin.

48 PRETZELS

1 oz. [2 tablespoons] plus 1 teaspoon butter
½ oz. fresh yeast
¼ teaspoon sugar
8 fl. oz. [1 cup] lukewarm milk
12 oz. [3 cups] flour
½ teaspoon salt
1 tablespoon caraway seeds
1 egg, lightly beaten
2 teaspoons coarse sea salt

With the teaspoon of butter, grease two large baking sheets and set aside.

Crumble the yeast into a small bowl and mash in the sugar with a kitchen fork. Add 2 tablespoons of the lukewarm milk and cream the milk and yeast together. Set the bowl aside in a warm, draught-free place for 15 to 20 minutes or until the yeast mixture is puffed up and frothy.

Meanwhile, in a small saucepan, melt the remaining butter in the remaining milk over low heat. Remove the pan from the heat and allow the milk mixture to cool to lukewarm.

Sift the flour and salt into a warmed, large mixing bowl. Add 2 teaspoons of the caraway seeds to the flour mixture. Make a well in the centre and pour in the yeast and milk and butter mixtures. Using your fingers or a spatula, gradually draw the flour mixture into the liquid. Continue mixing until all the flour is incorporated and the dough comes away from the sides of the bowl.

Turn the dough out on to a lightly floured board or marble slab and knead it for 8 minutes, reflouring the surface if the

Serve these crunchy German Pretzels with pre-dinner drinks.

dough becomes sticky. The dough should be smooth and elastic.

Rinse, thoroughly dry and lightly grease the large mixing bowl. Shape the dough into a ball and return it to the bowl. Cover the bowl with a clean damp cloth and set it in a warm, draught-free place for 45 minutes or until the dough has risen slightly.

Turn the risen dough out of the bowl on to a floured surface and knead it for 4 minutes.

Using your hands, form the dough into a roll 12-inches long. Cut the roll into 48 equal pieces with a knife. Roll out each piece of dough into a thin sausage shape, about 6-inches long. Place each dough piece on a working surface and curve the ends toward yourself. Cross the loop half-way along each side and twist once. Bend the ends back and press them firmly on to the curve of the loop.

Preheat the oven to fairly hot 375°F (Gas Mark 5, 190°C).

Half-fill a large saucepan with boiling water and bring the water to the boil again over moderately high heat. Drop the dough pieces into the water, a few at a time. Cook for 1 minute or until they rise to the surface of the water. Using a slotted spoon, remove the pieces from the pan and drain them in a colander. Cook the remaining dough in the same way. Put the pretzels on the baking sheets.

Using a pastry brush, coat each dough piece with the beaten egg, and sprinkle it with the remaining caraway seeds and the sea salt.

Place the baking sheets in the oven and bake the pretzels for 15 minutes or until they are golden brown and firm to the touch.

Remove the baking sheets from the oven and transfer the pretzels to a wire rack to cool completely.

Either serve immediately or store until required.

Bread and Butter Pudding

A perennial British favourite, Bread and Butter Pudding is easy and economical to make and delicious to eat. Its custard-like consistency is attractive to children.

3 TO 4 SERVINGS

1 teaspoon butter, softened
6 thin slices of white bread, crusts removed and liberally buttered
3 oz. [¾ cup] seedless raisins
½ teaspoon grated nutmeg
2 tablespoons sugar

CUSTARD

2 eggs
15 fl. oz. [1⅞ cups] milk

1 tablespoon sugar
½ teaspoon vanilla essence

Grease the bottom and sides of a medium-sized, shallow baking dish with the butter.

Cut the slices of bread into quarters. Place a layer of bread (buttered side up) on the bottom of the dish and sprinkle with half the raisins, nutmeg and 1 table-spoon sugar.

Add a second layer of bread and sprinkle on the rest of the raisins, nut-meg and sugar. Top with a final layer of bread, buttered side up.

To make the custard, beat the eggs in a large mixing bowl with a wire whisk. Heat the milk, sugar and vanilla essence. Add the heated milk mixture to the eggs, beating continuously to combine the ingredients well. Strain the mixture over the bread and let stand for at least 30 minutes, or until the bread has absorbed most of the liquid.

Preheat the oven to fairly hot 375°F (Gas Mark 5, 190°C).

Place the pudding in the centre of the oven and bake for 35 to 45 minutes, or until the top is crisp and golden.

Danish Pastries

These miraculously light, layered pastries are easily made with a yeast dough which is rolled in the same way as puff pastry. They can be cut into many different shapes, or made into turnovers, and flavoured with any or all of the fillings suggested. Serve them with afternoon coffee or as a dessert.

12-15 PASTRIES

1 oz. fresh yeast
1 teaspoon sugar
5 fl. oz. [⅝ cup] milk, warmed
1 lb. [4 cups] flour
1 teaspoon salt
1 teaspoon ground cardamom
2 oz. [¼ cup] castor sugar
10 oz. [1¼ cups] butter
2 eggs

GLAZE

1 egg, lightly beaten
4 tablespoons icing [confectioners'] sugar mixed with 2 tablespoons hot water (optional)

FILLING

2 crisp eating apples
1 teaspoon lemon juice
4 tablespoons apricot jam

Crumble the yeast into a small bowl. Add the sugar and 2 to 3 tablespoons of the milk and, with a fork, mash together to form a paste. Set the bowl aside in a warm, draught-free place for 15 to 20 minutes or until the yeast mixture is puffed up

For combs, cut the pastry into squares, place the filling in the centre and fold in half. Make slits.

For pinwheels, cut the pastry into a large rectangle, spread the dough with the filling, roll up and slice.

For stars, cut the pastry into squares, make cuts at each corner and fold four points to the centre.

For triangles, cut the pastry into squares, place the filling in the centre and fold diagonally.

and frothy.

Sift the flour, salt, ground cardamom and castor sugar into a large bowl. Add 2 ounces [¼ cup] of the butter and cut it into small pieces with a table knife. With your fingertips, rub the butter into the flour mixture until the mixture resembles fine breadcrumbs. Add the yeast mixture, the remaining milk and the eggs to the mixture. Mix well to make a soft dough (add more milk if necessary). Cover the bowl with a cloth and place it in the refrigerator to chill for 10 minutes.

Allow the remaining butter to soften slightly and form it into an oblong about 9- x 5-inches.

Turn the dough out on to a floured board and knead it lightly until it becomes smooth and elastic. Roll it out to an oblong about 12- x 8-inches. Place the butter in the centre and fold the edges of the dough over to completely enclose the butter. Roll out the dough to a strip about 5- x 15-inches. Fold the bottom third up and the top third down. Cover the dough and place it in the refrigerator to rest for 10 minutes. Repeat the rolling process twice more. Cover the dough and leave it in the refrigerator while making the filling.

Peel, core and thinly slice the apples into a small mixing bowl. Sprinkle over the lemon juice. Stir in the apricot jam.

To shape the pastries, remove the dough from the refrigerator and turn it out on to a lightly floured board. Roll out the dough to ¼-inch thick and cut it into 3-inch squares. Place about 1 teaspoon of filling in the centre of each square and brush the edges with the beaten egg. Fold the pastry in half to make either rectangular or triangular shapes. Alternatively, bring the corners to the centre and press them together.

Preheat the oven to hot 425°F (Gas Mark 7, 220°C).

After all the pastries have been shaped, place them on baking sheets and leave them in a warm, draught-free place to prove for 20 to 30 minutes.

Glaze them again with beaten egg and place the baking sheets in the oven. Bake the pastries for 15 minutes.

Remove the baking sheets from the oven and transfer the pastries to a wire rack. When they are cool, if you like, coat them with the sugar and water glaze.

Danish Pastries with Almond Filling

Prepare the Danish pastry dough and

place it in the refrigerator to chill for 10 minutes.

In a small mixing bowl, cream 1 tablespoon of butter with 3 ounces [⅜ cup] of castor sugar. Add 3 ounces [½ cup] ground almonds, 2 to 3 drops of almond essence and ½ lightly beaten egg. Stir to make a firm paste.

Roll out the pastry and cut it into 3-inch squares. Place a teaspoon of the filling in the centre of each square and shape and bake the pastries as in the basic recipe.

Danish Pastries with Cinnamon Sugar Filling

Prepare the Danish pastry dough and

place it in the refrigerator to chill for 10 minutes.

In a small mixing bowl, cream 2 ounces [¼ cup] of butter with 2 ounces [¼ cup] of castor sugar and stir in 2 teaspoons ground cinnamon and 2 tablespoons raisins.

Roll out the pastry and cut it into 3-inch squares. Place a teaspoon of the filling in the centre of each square and shape and bake the pastries as in the basic recipe. Once you have mastered the method, you will have lots of fun devising your own fillings. For pineapple and banana filling, chop 4 ounces canned pineapple, drained, and mix with 2 chopped bananas and 1 tablespoon of lemon juice. Place a teaspoon in the centre of each square and bake.

Index